Immersive Technologies to Accelerate Innovation

Smart Innovation Set

coordinated by
Dimitri Uzunidis

Volume 38

Immersive Technologies to Accelerate Innovation

How Virtual and Augmented Reality Enables the Co-Creation of Concepts

Sylvain Fleury
Simon Richir

iSTE

WILEY

First published 2021 in Great Britain and the United States by ISTE Ltd and John Wiley & Sons, Inc.

ISTE Ltd
27-37 St George's Road
London SW19 4EU
UK

www.iste.co.uk

John Wiley & Sons, Inc.
111 River Street
Hoboken, NJ 07030
USA

www.wiley.com

Library of Congress Control Number: 2021943895

British Library Cataloguing-in-Publication Data
A CIP record for this book is available from the British Library
ISBN 978-1-78630-770-5

MIX
Paper from responsible sources
FSC® C013604

Contents

Foreword

The need for change in a company often translates into a real need to adapt in order to survive, especially in a constrained environment; in other words, it is a matter of innovating or dying. This was well illustrated during recent crises, for example in 2008 with the financial crisis, when, even under reduced resources, the accelerated change toward an "open innovation" model with external partners, academics, customers and suppliers, enabled us to prepare for the rebound after the crisis. More recently, during the Covid-19 pandemic in 2020, the rapid use of digitalization and the electrification of transport are already preparing us for environmental challenges, particularly related to global warming and the necessary reduction in the use of fossil fuels. In this changing world, the innovation process facilitates change and creates a positive, continuous and visible dynamic. This process is useful for companies to focus efforts at the right time, with the right intensity, in the right place, with competent and prepared teams. The notions of market and temporality are also crucial. Without a market, innovation will only remain at the invention stage, an expense for the company with no return on investment. To be successful, this implies a continuous intimacy with customers, a shared value creation process. The innovation process must also adapt to the context and make the most of available technologies, wherever they may be, from our suppliers, our academic partners, and public or private research. The meeting with the teams working at the Laval Virtual Center and the work carried out with the *Institut Arts et Métiers de Laval* have enabled MANN+HUMMEL, a leading global company in filtration technology, to strengthen its strategy in the field of digitalization, by seeking to create value from digital data, and by applying it to the innovation process. The speed with which we can interact with our customers in our ideation processes, up to the realization of prototypes, real or virtual, is an important factor in convincing future customers, investors and internal or external decision makers. In 2016, based on this observation, the collaboration between MANN+HUMMEL and the *Institut Arts et Métiers de Laval* was initiated in order to conduct research and experimentation on the contribution of technology, related to virtual reality, to the innovation process. This project is called "Time to Concept", and its objective is to reduce the time between ideation and the first customer experience. It is about putting the user or the customer at the center of the game by immersing them, gathering their emotions and feedback, and taking these into account in real time to adapt the product or the service. It is also of course about converging, at the end, on a creation of value, demonstrated in the virtual environment, with system interactions made more visible. For example, during a recent car show in Frankfurt, we managed to put a few customers under virtual reality headsets to gather their impressions of a new vehicle interior filtration system: a situation lasting less than two minutes to explain everything, in particular to visualize the invisible, that is, the improvement of the vehicle's air quality. Remembering the experience, one of them, a world-renowned car manufacturer, then selected us to create a demonstration vehicle. In the field of air quality improvement, which is one of the strategic axes of the MANN+HUMMEL Group, we try to make visible with the help of virtual reality the physical phenomena at stake, such as fluid mechanics, the propagation of pollutants and their filtration. Explaining them is all the more necessary to bring to the market new and more efficient filtration technologies, adapted to the new uses of mobility and our lifestyles, and also in tune with the new recommendations and regulations in this field. Thus, this book describes the generic results of research work validated in concrete cases to support the digital transformation of innovation within companies through immersive technologies.

Jérôme Migaud
Transportation Innovation Director
at MANN+HUMMEL Group

September 2021

Acknowledgments

We would like to thank our industrial partners for providing us with study sites and opportunities to evaluate the methods described in this book in real-life situations. In particular, we would like to thank MANN+HUMMEL for their contribution through the financing of the Time to Concept Chair, which has given rise to a number of the research projects presented in this book. We think in particular of Jérôme Migaud, Bruno Langer, Philippe Rhoumy and Luc De Keyser. Our thanks go to the *Arts et Métiers* Foundation for its support to the Chair, in particular Gilbert Paulezec and Roger Stanchina, but also Aurélien Agnès who supported us for 1 year in this scientific program. Of course, we would like to thank the representatives of the steering committee of the Time to Concept Chair: Jean Quessada, Ivan Iordanoff, Alexandre Rigal, Xavier Château and Xavier Kestelyn.

We would also like to thank Charles Mille for the numerous exchanges that contributed to the reflections on the methods and tools, and also Thibaut Guitter and Benjamin Poussard for their participation in the research work and the design of the virtual reality tools, as well as Marie-Pierre Verrier for preparing the numerous communication and scientific sharing events that punctuated this program.

Numerous scientific collaborations with researchers from our team or outside have also contributed to this work, in particular Olivier Christmann, Geoffrey Gorisse, Philippe Blanchard, Marc Pallot and Laurent Dupont.

The students of the MTI3D Master's at the *Institut Arts et Métiers de Laval* contributed to this work by realizing some of the technology elements presented in this book.

Finally, thanks to Laurent Chrétien and the great team of Laval Virtual for their logistical support and for the regular exchanges on the uses of immersive technologies that have stimulated our creativity over the years.

September 2021

Preface

In this book, we regularly refer to research work conducted by our team at the *Institut Arts et Métiers de Laval.* It is therefore not superfluous to provide a few elements of context beforehand.

The *École Nationale Supérieure d'Arts et Métiers* is a French engineering school renowned for its orientation toward the industrial world. The *Institut de Laval,* attached to the Angers campus, has developed in conjunction with the Laval virtual reality ecosystem and in particular Laval Virtual, the organizers of the international virtual reality trade show. The institute manages the MTI3D master's degree, which trains high-level students in the management and engineering of immersive technologies. The Institute's researchers form the "presence and innovation" team of the "*Laboratoire Arts et Métiers ParisTech d'Angers*" (LAMPA). The work of the team concerns not only virtual reality, user experience and use cases of virtual reality in different industrial sectors (training, health, product design, etc.) but also innovation methods and creativity. Alongside research activities, the team is led to support companies in their adoption of immersive technologies and also in their innovation processes, notably through the animation of creativity workshops.

Within the framework of the Chair entitled Time to Concept, a series of work has been completed on immersive technologies for ideation. This work has enabled the formalization and evaluation of the Time to Concept method described in this book. It is therefore both a researcher's viewpoint that is proposed and the result of a field experience built on the basis of tests and regular feedback in real situations.

September 2021

Introduction

Humanity has always sought to innovate by inventing new products, services or manufacturing processes. Innovation is part of our DNA. The Renaissance (14th–16th centuries) was a period of greatness. Five hundred years later, we are now living in the "Renaissance 2.0", a new period of major innovations, both great and troubled, that history will remember.

Collective intelligence, boosted by increasing network speeds and artificial intelligence, gives rise to new ideas every second across the planet. Like comets, most of these ideas fade away as quickly as they appeared, before being transformed into intelligible concepts that can be seized by the companies best equipped for innovation.

The digital transformation of companies is a competitive challenge and a complex step for large groups and industries, but at the same time a tremendous opportunity. This transformation is moving into another dimension with the development of immersive technologies and artificial intelligence. The challenge of innovation and digital transformation are now coming together as more and more research shows the potential of immersive technologies in accelerating the first steps in the innovation process.

1

Innovation Management: Issues and Key Points for a Vital and Strategic Process

Systematic innovation requires a willingness
to see change as an opportunity.
PETER DRUCKER

1.1. A question of survival

Every year since 1955, *Fortune* magazine has published a ranking of the 500 highest-grossing U.S. companies. In 2014, the *American Enterprise Institute* revealed that 88% of the companies initially included in this ranking were no longer in existence. Some had gone bankrupt, others were bought out, even though most of them had been flagships of American industry. As Joseph Schumpeter said, most companies die "of old age" when they are no longer able to innovate. Lack of innovation naturally leads established companies to disappear. These disappearances are accelerated by the arrival of new companies which, on the contrary, are born and develop in their wake. Innovation is therefore a question of survival, or at least of maintaining a dominant position.

1.1.1. *The example of Blockbuster Video*

Blockbuster Video is a famous example of a company that died of old age due to lack of innovation. Founded in 1985 in Dallas, the company operated a chain of VHS movie rental stores. It adapted to the evolution of video media, moving from VHS to DVD and video games. In 2000, Blockbuster had an option to buy the young California company Netflix for $50 million. Blockbuster's executive at the time refused the deal because Netflix was losing money. In 2014, Blockbuster Video went bankrupt while Netflix raked in more than $5 billion in annual revenue. Netflix made all video rental companies obsolete in a few years. Blockbuster Video, in a dominant position, failed to make the paradigm shift that was needed at the time. The story was not over, as in 2019 and 2020, no less than six competing platforms came to the market with a technological and economic model similar to that of Netflix: Disney, NBC, Apple, HBO and Amazon. There is also room for "followers"; it is never too late to innovate.

1.1.2. *A regime of intensive innovation*

The challenge of innovation is to survive or to maintain one's advantageous position. This is not new, of course, but innovation is even more crucial today than it was yesterday because we have entered a regime of intensive innovation (Hatchuel *et al.* 2000). On a global scale, the number of patents filed and scientific publications is constantly increasing. While it took more than 60 years to go from a 17 cm vinyl to a 12 cm CD, it took only 5 years to go from a digital music player to a subscription-based streaming service. This example illustrates the accelerating pace of innovation. MPO, the European leader in vinyl records, became the European leader in CDs and then DVDs after a successful technological transition. Moreover, the reduction in the number of vinyl records on the shelves has not disrupted the expertise of companies in this field, whereas the arrival of online listening platforms has made other media obsolete. This is the second characteristic of the era of intensive innovation: innovation is increasingly radical. Not only do disruptions happen more often, but they are also more brutal. Companies are therefore more and more subject to the risk of seeing their market disrupted and must adopt methods that allow them to transform this risk into an opportunity. Incremental innovation remains essential, but does not protect against the emergence of a disruptive competitor.

It is possible to prepare oneself to face this obligation of innovation, either through methods or tools. Innovation is a way of transforming ourselves to absorb the revolutions underway; the digital revolution in the broadest sense (including artificial intelligence, immersive technologies, supercomputers, etc.) is the one we are currently dealing with. It is also a way to adapt to the new constraints linked to the consideration of ecological issues, with a set of opportunities to be seized.

The impact of innovation as a process is considerable in the long run, but innovations as an outcome of the process are often small, incremental steps. We only hear the stories of very dramatic innovation, but most innovations are not. They are not original, nor technically complex, and often look like common sense in hindsight.

1.1.3. *From creativity to innovation*

Creativity differs from innovation in that the former is about coming up with ideas and the latter is about implementing them. Creativity is therefore a psychological trait and process, whereas innovation is a management issue, a professional activity that is generally collective. Indeed, the implementation of ideas often requires the association of several forms of expertise in an innovation team. When the organization allows it, creativity will generate a flow of new ideas that will feed the innovation process. If innovation is a question of survival, it is also an exciting playground with flexible rules, allowing each step forward to transform ideas into successes. The challenge is to ensure that new ideas can survive in mature companies, that is, with an optimized organization for production and continuous improvement but whose rigidity sometimes blocks any possibility of radical innovation (Lecossier *et al.* 2018). As a result, mature companies need to redesign their innovation process to protect truly innovative ideas as they mature. A survey by the Product

Development and Management Association reveals that 24% of companies with a true innovation methodology manage to bring one out of every four generated ideas to fruition, while 76% of companies with fewer tools bring only one out of every nine to fruition.

Figure 1.1. *It is essential to train in methods to improve the innovation process, to protect ideas, to have a dedicated place and to train teams in ideation methods. For a color version of this figure, see www.iste.co.uk/fleury/innovation.zip*

1.1.4. *Equipping ourselves to innovate better*

It is necessary to be equipped with new technologies to take advantage of recent advances in the field. The time it takes for a company to go from idea to concept is the key factor. The revolution that is taking place in the world of immersive technologies is a tremendous opportunity to accelerate innovation. Today, immersive tools for innovation are emerging. It is now a question of seizing them and conceiving the uses that will allow us to make the most of them to innovate.

In many companies, innovation processes are clearly defined and standardized, with sequenced phases, from idea gathering to transfer to development and then production units.

Virtual technologies, which are now mature, can provide a decisive advantage in accelerating the processes put in place, by equipping specific phases of this process. Thus, virtual and augmented reality, while it has already proven its benefit for product design, can be used from the creative phases and integrated into the digital chain to facilitate the production of intermediate representations, whether virtual or physical, as in the case of three-dimensional (3D) printing.

To support innovation, these technologies must be embedded in an organization. They must be introduced in a timely and appropriate manner in terms of management. They will be employed by users who will rely on them to be more creative. These technologies must therefore also be compatible with the cognitive characteristics of the users to encourage their creativity.

The purpose of this book is not to describe in detail what immersive technologies are. Our position as researchers in a laboratory specialized in innovation and immersive technologies leads us to support companies in their digital transition and to help them optimize their innovation processes. We show our support (e.g. in our creativity workshops) with virtual reality technologies, notably thanks to the immersive applications developed in our laboratory. We are convinced (and we have a lot of scientific proof) that this way of doing innovation constitutes a considerable gain in efficiency and will progressively impose itself in companies that have the desire to innovate. The objective of this book is to provide elements concerning the uses of these technologies for innovation. The research works that are called upon are therefore often at the frontier of, or totally within, the human sciences, but also from the design sciences. An individual alone is not innovative. At best, an individual can be creative. It is the conjunction of the creativity of a whole multidisciplinary team that leads to innovation. Innovation management consists of creating an organizational, human and possibly technological environment that is as favorable as possible to innovation.

1.1.5. *Modeling innovation at the company level*

Numerous models exist which outline the innovation process, that is, the stages located before the industrialization of a product, which we will call the upstream phases of design. Several of these models take the form of a funnel, wide on the left and thin on the right, to graphically represent a large number of ideas at the beginning and successive selection stages as concepts are developed. This is the case, for example, with the innovation funnel model or the innovation pipeline. Innovation opportunities are generated from the company's strategy, prospective analyses, market studies, or the company's existing or future know-how. Then, the ideas are refined, filtered, merged, to disappear or evolve into a more complete form, the concept. The concepts are then transformed and developed according to the feasibility constraints to be industrialized and then become marketable products.

Bouchard *et al.* (2006) have modeled product design in the context of work on innovation in the automotive sector. This approach concerns a process in which the designer's creativity will potentially concern innovative uses or functions, but also esthetic choices. This innovation process is composed of three main successive steps: inspiration, generation and embodiment. Inspiration corresponds to the exploration process which consists of gathering data concerning the context of the future product in order to converge on first guidelines. This can take the form of a moodboard that will be used to inspire the designers during the following stages. The second step, generation, is a divergence phase during which the designer will create representations of the product through sketches. Finally, embodiment consists of converging, that is, selecting the best concepts, refining them until they are finally put into production.

1.2. The blue ocean strategy

The traditional approach is to face a known market in which companies compete violently for market share against each other on a roughly constant demand. This is the red ocean strategy. The ocean is red with the blood generated by this violence. It is also red with the color of the companies' accounts. In this red ocean, decisions are made based on the competition. The advantage is that you know the market; you know it exists and you know its main characteristics. So it is a question of exploiting the existing demand, of beating the competitors, either by obtaining a better quality-price ratio or by differentiating oneself.

The blue ocean strategy described in the book *Blue Ocean Strategy* (Mauborgne and Kim 2007) is about moving away from an obsession with confrontation and instead seeking to create virgin markets. It is about creating trends rather than adapting to established trends. In the blue ocean, the company is not caught in competitive wars because it is the only one there. The new market does not necessarily require a technological innovation; it can be a service innovation as long as it creates value for both the company and the buyer. These innovations that create both profitability for the company and usefulness for the customer are called "useful" innovations. The blue oceans are therefore made up of all the activities in which there is not yet a competitive confrontation because they have not yet been developed, or because only one player has positioned itself there. In the blue oceans, there are many opportunities for strong and rapid growth. Logically, each blue ocean discovered by an innovative company ends up becoming a red ocean because of the arrival of competitors with an imitation strategy.

The creation of a blue ocean market should not be confused with technological innovation. Technological innovation is certainly a factor in the development of markets, but it is not necessarily the central determinant of the appearance of a new market. It is easy to find many examples of companies that have created new markets without technological innovation being the driving force:

– Starbucks, for example, corresponds only to a new use;

– Uber is technologically only a mobile application.

Conversely, a truly technologically innovative product may not open up a new market if it is not acceptable, useful, fun or easy to use.

Google Glasses[1] were probably not a bad idea in themselves, but the technological ecosystem may not have been mature enough and there were some issues that made them unacceptable (discreet video recording, for example).

The companies that manage to go into a blue ocean are those that are successful in creating value by innovating. This value creation can come from a simplification of something that already exists, from a gain in time, productivity, pleasure, meaning, etc. In any case, technological innovation is only one way to open a market.

The blue ocean strategy should not be confused with differentiation. Differentiation consists mainly of making trade-offs on cost and service. Overall, it is about doing the same thing as a competitor, but cheaper or more high-end. Of course, when we create a low-cost equivalent of a product, we enlarge the potential customer base. However, if we have an effect on the market, we cannot say that we are really opening a new market in this case. Creating a new market is not about making a trade-off between quality and cost. It is not about being different from others, but about doing better. The limitation of this strategy is that even when a company manages to find a blue ocean, the advantage it gains is only temporary because other companies will quickly come along to take market share. In a way, the company that opened the market is the one that took all the risks, while those that follow have the ground already cleared in front of them.

1.3. Open innovation

Open innovation is an innovation management technique theorized in the early 2000s by Henry Chesbrough, a research professor at the University of Berkley. He did not invent this approach, but grouped under the name "open innovation" practices that he saw emerging in more and more companies. This is a mode of organization in which people outside the R&D department and possibly outside the company take part directly in the innovation process. This type of approach can

---

1 Augmented reality glasses project, which was abandoned in 2015.

be in tension with the widespread culture of secrecy in the field of innovation, since each company wants to avoid its competitors being able to anticipate or copy the innovations it is going to produce. Practicing open innovation therefore requires dealing with intellectual property issues upstream and with rigor.

1.3.1. *The two types of open innovation*

We classically identify two main categories of open innovation: inside-out and outside-in (Chesbrough 2003). Inside-out open innovation starts with a desire to apply a company's technology to other markets in order to increase the return on investment or to anticipate a change in the market. For a large company, it is a matter of putting in place a small team to develop an area that does not fit into the global strategy. Extracting a team through a business creation allows us to benefit from the agility of a small company to find a new market. The best known example of inside-out is Adobe, which came about from a team from the Xerox research institute.

Outside-in open innovation is mobilized in cases where the company has a specific need for a skill or expertise that it does not possess internally. This may concern, for example, the desire to understand the opportunities and risks associated with the emergence of a new technology on the market. Typically, companies in sectors such as retail or insurance have seen the emergence of artificial intelligence for several years, and feel that this is likely to disrupt their business, constituting both a risk and an opportunity. In this case, they will look for external resources to innovate in this direction, because internal R&D is not specialized in this type of technology and will not be able to identify the opportunities. It can also concern the need to solve a technological or scientific problem for which the company does not have the internal expertise. In this case, open innovation is a way for the company to find external resources. This can take the form, for example, of numerous innovation competitions aimed at start-ups or hackathons in which groups of students must propose solutions to a problem encountered by the company.

In some cases, outside-in open innovation is not about generating ideas from expertise, but rather about having ideas selected by the community. For example, a company looking to quickly renew its product line can gather the community's opinion to prioritize the products to be developed while being sure that they will meet consumer expectations.

1.3.2. *The example of the MayAM challenge*

For many years, our laboratory has organized the MayAM (for "*Mayenne-Arts et Métiers*") open innovation challenge with groups of students from the *Institut des Arts et Métiers de Laval* specialized in immersive technologies. Each group of students is assigned an industrial company wishing to seize opportunities related to virtual and augmented reality technologies. They must then work for a week to imagine an innovative project for the company. The participating companies are part of an outside-in open innovation approach in the sense that they do not have the internal expertise to identify the risks and opportunities related to these technologies. Therefore, through MayAM, they must find an external resource that will do this work for them. The next logical step in this process is to integrate an expert resource, often through an intern, or a support service provided by the laboratory or a company.

1.3.3. *Collaborative innovation*

The organization of companies in silos often leads to a very low circulation of ideas. Also, beyond the exploitation of external resources, many companies under-exploit internal expertise. This is a form of open innovation, but rather thought at the level of a department, which we call *collaborative innovation* and which consists of making the circulation of ideas throughout the company more fluid by mobilizing the expertise of other departments.

1.3.4. *Crowdsourcing*

Crowdsourcing is one of the classic tools of outside-in open innovation. The significant development of crowdsourcing in recent years is due to the rise of social networks that make it possible to create and manage communities around specific topics (Whitla 2009). The crowdsourcing process has been described by Trompette *et al.* (2008) as follows: the organization identifies an activity that it does not want to perform internally. Rather than outsource it in the traditional way, that is, have it performed by a service provider, the company chooses to crowdsource. In this case, it posts the specifications on the Internet (on a platform or on its own Website) and sets the terms of participation (schedule, remuneration, etc.). This allows a large number of individuals to work on the activity. The company then validates the contribution of each person, according to the specifications established in advance, and allocates the expected rewards.

1.3.5. *The lead user*

The lead user concept was developed by Von Hippel, an economist at the MIT Sloan School of Management. To understand who the lead users are, we need to go back to the mechanics of innovation diffusion described by Everett Roger. According to this approach, we consider that when a product is launched, we will first have a few users called "innovators" who are few in number, but interested enough in innovations that they are very easy to convince to buy an innovative product. Then come the "early adopters", who are a little more numerous and a little more resistant, although they are very interested in innovation, and so on, with the early majority, the late majority and finally the late adopters, who are only likely to be interested in an innovation when it is very widely diffused and established in society. In Von Hippel's conception, the lead users are the few individuals who are even further upstream than the innovators described by Everett Roger, that is even before the commercial release of the product.

Lead users have two important characteristics:

– they are ahead of the major trends in the evolution of uses and they recognize the needs before the others;

– they have an advantage and skills that lead them to innovate by themselves by developing the solution to their need.

Thus, lead users use prototypes to satisfy their needs before a commercial product can do so. In this sense, they are considered sources of innovation.

In theory, one might think that it is very easy to create radical innovations and always be one step ahead of the market by integrating lead users into the innovation process. In practice, we only know for sure that someone was ahead of the curve later on. Survivor syndrome, which is very common in the world of innovation, comes into play, giving us the opportunity to see the success of genius visionaries who "feel" the future and the evolutions to come. After the fact, it is safe to say that the founder of Oculus is a lead user and that the purchase of his company by Facebook to integrate it into its strategy is an illustrative success. It is a success, but let us not forget that it is because it was a success that this case is famous. In any case, lead users are often opinion leaders in their field because of their very strong expertise.

To identify lead users in a given field of activity, Von Hippel described a method called "pyramid". It involves asking experts who they think are the best experts in the field, then going to them and asking the same question, and so on until you have a workable list of five or six names of people to interview who will be at the top. You have potentially got your hands on some lead users in your field! The next step is to analyze the usage of these few specialists and identify the types of technologies they use to meet the needs you want to address. If their usage leads you to other areas of expertise, you can then repeat the process of identifying lead users in these other areas of expertise.

1.4. Technical and human issues from ideation to design

The innovation process not only is based on methods but also relies on tools that can vary according to the type of project, its progress or the habits of the company.

Technology is the natural partner of the designer, especially when it comes to representing previously identified concepts. Indeed, most of the time, the digital representation tools are not mobilized during the ideation. The generation of ideas is classically carried out in textual form on Post-it notes or a paperboard, in the form of sketches, or by creating physical models with materials that are malleable or can be assembled such as modeling clay, cardboard or Lego (Dorta 2004). Computer-based 3D tools are usually reserved for later stages. In the design process, they are actually used to represent ideas that have already been selected and developed.

1.4.1. *The sketch as a reflective process*

After the very first phases of divergent ideation, the designer will use two types of "conversation": a conversation with self and a conversation with co-designers and clients. Both types of conversation will require both visual representations and fluidity in the execution of the representation of the designer's ideas.

The designer's conversation with self refers to what Dorta (2004) calls reflection-in-action, which could be called a "reflective" conversation. In this process, the designer externalizes mental images, represents and represents again, producing new discoveries at each iteration that will lead to new ideas. They need external representations that are rather imprecise, focused on the important concepts, in order to interact with their own mental representations. They will be in continuous interaction with their representations to make design decisions (Visser 2006). The process thus consists of alternating actions and judgments. The designer's actions can produce unexpected results; the feedback is likely to suggest concepts. Tools that encourage spontaneity, that is, natural gestures and letting go, are the most likely to generate feedback and will then tend to stimulate reflection, reflective conversation, and thus improve ideation (Schön 1983). An external representation constructed in a design process is considered to be a cognitive artifact of designing (Visser 2006) in the sense that this artifact contains knowledge, or at least information that is intended to be re-mobilized by the designer or their partners. When the designer does not have the experience to mentally visualize and solve design problems, or when the problem is too complex, these cognitive artifacts are essential to the ideation process.

1.4.2. *Types of representation*

Reflective conversation will generally be more important in the early stages of design. Goel (1995) describes the design process as an evolution of different types of representations. For each stage, a particular type of representation is used for specific tasks. During the ideation stage, a first type of representation consisting of freehand sketches or physical models is mobilized to externalize and visualize design intentions or to communicate them with others. These first representations are what Goldschmidt (1992) calls idea-sketches. Later in the process, presentation sketches appear, in the form of digital 3D models, drawings or images, to improve communicating asynchronously with colleagues and clients about the proposals. At the end of the process appear the representations composed of detailed technical drawings and rapid prototyping models to communicate the exact and definitive information to build the product. During these three successive steps, the representations are likely to be mobilized during synchronous, but especially asynchronous collaborations with other designers or customers. For example, team ideation requires cognitive artifacts adapted to different visualization capacities, and these artifacts must also be manipulated in an intuitive way.

The design process is based on the creation of different forms of representations (Goel 1995). It is an iterative process in which designers propose and analyze forms to achieve identified functions. The generation of these forms depends on the designers' abilities to create internal, mental and external visualizations (Cross and Roy 1989). Drawing is thus a key function of design, and the role of this activity evolves throughout the process. Drawing allows the designer to transform ideas into concepts, thus conceptualizing (Cross and Roy 1989; Ullman *et al.* 1990), to make these concepts communicable, and then to specify technical details (Bertoline 1999). Sketching allows designers to change their level of abstraction, expand their short-term memory to facilitate problem solving (Ullman 2003) and improve their exploration processes that are essential to understanding (Cross 1999).

The traditional engineering approach is to consider the drawing on paper as a draft that will be followed by work on a Computer-Aided Design (CAD) tool. However, there are certain restrictions imposed by CAD tools that, in the early stages of design, will hinder creativity, especially by generating fixation. The importance of sketching as a means of supporting visual reasoning was first highlighted in 1980 by McKim, who spoke of idea-sketching. Indeed, the designer's conceptualization activity is limited, in particular, by his or her memory capacities. On average, short-term memory is limited to seven chunks of information (Miller 1956). In the case of the design of a technical object, a chunk corresponds to a characteristic of the product. Technical experts in this product category are then able to put more information in each chunk than novices (Ullman 2003). The quick sketch, the idea-sketch, is a way to externalize these chunks, making these sketches an extension of short-term memory. Thus, improving sketching skills, or improving the sketching tool, will help to store more information through these visualizations and will thus reduce the duration of the ideation phase.

1.4.3. *Conditions for the effectiveness of sketches*

Sketches in a design project, to be effective, must possess a number of characteristics identified by Buxton (2007):

– *quick to achieve*, so as not to interfere with the creative process;

– *done at the right time*, sketches are useful when a designer needs to externalize a mental representation, for a reflective conversation, or to communicate their ideas, preferably in the upstream phases of design;

– *inexpensive*, because it is a matter of allowing for mistakes, corrections, changes of ideas, adjustments;

– *disposable*, the investment in a sketch is the concept and not the sketch itself (normally, several sketches are made quickly and all of them are kept, which implies that one should never find a sketch by itself);

– *understandable*, because the communicability of the idea depends on it;

– characterized by the *freedom of the gesture*, neither tightened nor too precise;

– *minimalist*, only what is important to the concept, because technical details are distractors that tend to interfere with the ideation work (Rodgers *et al.* 2000);

– *with the appropriate degree of development*; the sketch's degree of development should match the idea's degree of development so that designers are not fixated on details of the idea rather than its central features;

– *suggesting rather than telling*, because the sketch is not the technical specification document that appears much later in CAD; suggesting leaves the user of the sketch a share of deductions to make, which may be conducive to finding solutions;

– *intentionally ambiguous*, as one should not, in seeking to represent a specific concept on an object, fix all of the other characteristics of that object. It is better to remain ambiguous about those features of the object that are not central to this sketch (Tseng and Ball 2011).

1.4.4. *The phases of ideation*

Dorta's (2004) and Goldschmidt's (1992) work highlights two main phases in ideation, corresponding to different constraints: the reflection-in-action phase, during which the designer needs tools that allow him or her to represent his or her ideas quickly and with natural gestures, even if this leads to a very imprecise result. For this purpose, the traditional tools used are paper and pencils, whether in the form of Post-it notes, flip charts or notepads. As we will detail later, virtual reality tools such as Time2Sketch are particularly well suited to this phase since they allow freehand 3D drawings to be made quickly and easily in the appropriate virtual environment. The second phase concerns the asynchronous collaboration, and implies that the designer realizes one or several "presentation sketches", that is, more precise and communicable representations of their ideas. This phase is usually done with CAD software. However, among virtual reality tools, software such as Time2Teach – enabling 3D animations to be created quickly using integrating flows – and Time2Craft – a virtual reality CAD module – enable this design step to be accelerated.

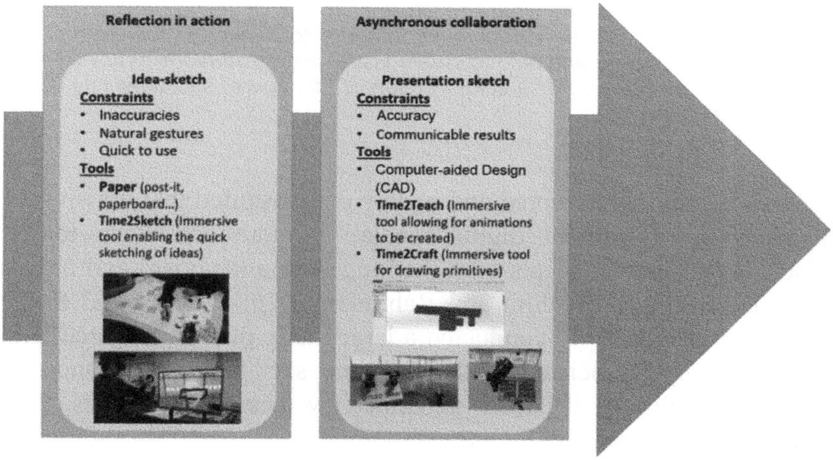

Figure 1.2. *Model of the upstream phase of design based on Dorta's (2004) phases and Goldschmidt's (1992) categories of sketches. For a color version of this figure, see www.iste.co.uk/fleury/innovation.zip*

1.4.5. *The right tools at the right time*

Robertson and Radcliffe (2009) have highlighted risks associated with using CAD software too early in the design process. It will tend to circumscribe thinking, create early fixation or "bounded" ideation. With CAD software, the designer does not want to back out of an idea because it involves relatively heavy technical actions. In other words, CAD can become an "innovation killer" if it is used too early and designers must be trained in terms of method to avoid this risk.

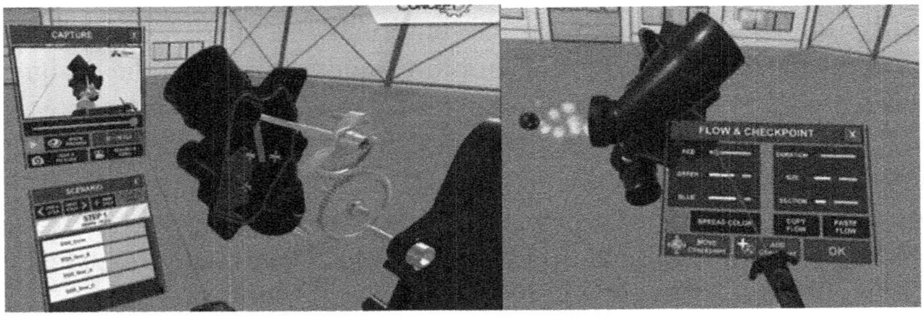

Figure 1.3. *Time2Teach: virtual reality tool for quickly and simply creating video animations, 3D or virtual environments to illustrate, for example, a mechanical operation, and also to create visual representations of flows (here, for example, air flows). For a color version of this figure, see www.iste.co.uk/fleury/innovation.zip*

It is commonly accepted and widely demonstrated that drawing by hand, with or without digital media, is more conducive to the discovery of new concepts than working with a keyboard and mouse (see, for example, Ibrahim and Rahimian 2010; Jackson and Keefe 2016). In our team, we conducted a large study that investigated both the creativity associated with different sketching tools and the communicability of the ideas generated by these tools, that is, their ability to be understood by partners (Mille *et al.* 2020). In this study, participants were asked to imagine improvements to be made to an umbrella so that it would also be useful when it was not raining. They had to imagine and draw as many ideas as possible that met this instruction in 15 minutes. They did this with each of the following four tools: paper/pencil, Time2Sketch, Google Blocks and SolidWork. The results indicate that participants generate on average more ideas when using paper/pencil or Time2Sketch than when using Google Blocks or SolidWork. In other words, they generate more ideas when the tool allows them to sketch freehand, in order to respect the natural gesture. On the other hand, Time2Sketch outperforms the other three conditions in terms of user experience, presumably because it combines the stimulating side of virtual reality with freehand use.

1.4.6. *A growing variety of tools*

Digital sketching is now a common practice to generate and communicate ideas during the ideation process. Devices on computers or smartphones create these types of sketches.

1.4.6.1. *Table, touch pad and pen*

Users can draw naturally as if they were using paper and pencil, reducing the time to create the sketch. The collaborative aspect is possible on touchscreen tablets where the screen is shared across multiple tablets (Pelland *et al.* 2019). Touchscreen tablets also allow for multi-user operation simultaneously, but directly on the same hardware. This opens up opportunities for users to replace the features of their pen with those of another medium, such as a paintbrush.

1.4.6.2. *Augmented reality on smartphones and tablets*

Augmented reality on smartphones and tablets is classically used to visualize an object in its future real environment, or to visualize transformations or information embedded on a real object.

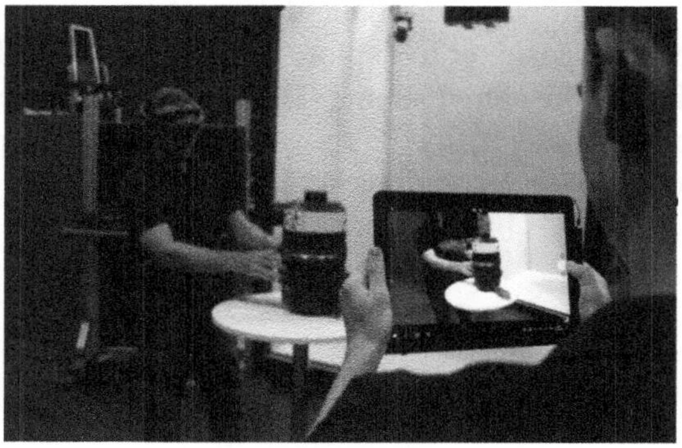

Figure 1.4. *Example of a collaborative work situation with augmented reality flow visualization (created with the Time2Teach virtual reality tool) on a tangible air filter, using a Hololens headset and a tablet. For a color version of this figure, see www.iste.co.uk/fleury/innovation.zip*

There are also apps available to create 3D sketches directly on tablets and smartphones. Combining 3D sketches with augmented reality can be a simple, inexpensive and effective solution for ideation (Pelland *et al.* 2019).

1.4.6.3. *Virtual reality sketches*

Virtual reality is used to create immersive models, in exterior or interior view, to present to project partners. It is possible to view a CAD model immersively, but there are also various programs that can create 3D models from virtual reality equipment. Generating concepts in 3D could be ideal for reducing the time until reaching the engineering process (Pelland *et al.* 2019). Gravity Sketch is one software package for users to work on 3D sketches. Time2Sketch is another example of software, developed by our team, that allows for multi-user sketch creation, among other things.

1.4.6.4. *Model generation by artificial intelligence*

Evolutionary algorithms are usually used to solve software engineering problems. Due to the success of these artificial intelligences, engineers have developed machine learning to calculate an ideal design for a problem with multiple variables. These machine-made digital designs are called "Generative Models". If these models are not yet able to provide satisfactory final designs, they can on the other hand propose automatic deformations on existing models in order to lead the designer to explore shapes that he or she would not necessarily have considered alone. This process requires significant computing power, and many hours of processing. Despite this, the generated models have an obvious potential for the future of design.

2

Creativity and Cognition: Factors and Biases of Mental Processes Involved in Creative Activities

Creativity is intelligence having fun.
ALBERT EINSTEIN

2.1. The creativity process

2.1.1. *The Wallas model (1926)*

While creativity has long been considered as a mystical phenomenon, taking different forms according to the times and culture, it has been studied for several decades as an intellectual process. Wallas (1926) was the first to formalize the creativity process.

The first step is preparation. It consists of analyzing the problem, collecting information and building knowledge about the problem. This stage is carried out consciously. The second step is incubation. The individual may be consciously working on the problem, or may have moved on to something else. However, incubation refers to the fact that consciously or unconsciously, the brain is still working on the problem by associating ideas. The third stage is illumination. This refers to the fact that suddenly a suitable idea comes to the individual's consciousness. It may emerge spontaneously from mental associations made unconsciously, or it may have been triggered by an external stimulus. The last step, verification, is conscious and deliberate, since it involves evaluating the validity of the idea in order to develop it. These four steps can take place in a linear way, but they can also go back and forth. For example, I may do several preparation/incubation loops before reaching illumination. Thus, the organization of projects should take into account the fact that creativity is a process that takes place over time. It is therefore important to present the problem to be solved early enough to allow time for incubation during other activities and not to pose a problem just before the deadline. The efficiency of each of the different stages can be modulated by the characteristics of the individuals, the organization, the methods and tools used or the location. For example, if the preparation stage requires concentration and therefore an absence of interference (noise, interruptions), the incubation stage of an idea is more effective when the level of cognitive load is at an intermediate level (Baird *et al.* 2012). This means that during the incubation phase, participants should perform a mental activity that requires a moderate level of concentration.

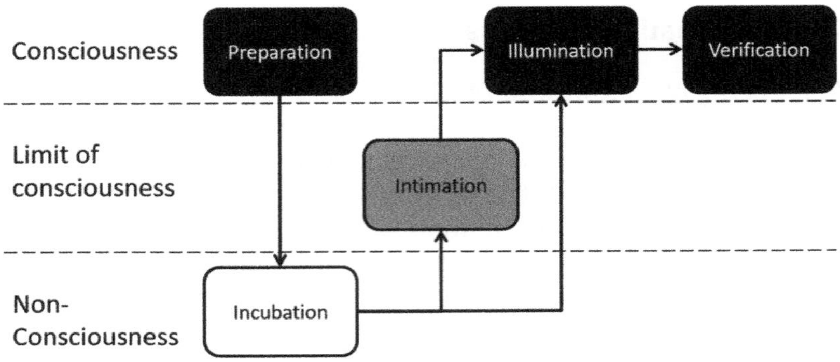

Figure 2.1. *Representation of the creativity process as a function of the corresponding level (Wallas 1926)*

2.1.2. *The GENEPLORE*

Other models of creativity have emerged, highlighting different aspects of the process. The GENEPLORE model (contraction of "generate" and "explore") describes the creative process as a succession of iterations between an idea generation activity and an exploration activity (see Figure 2.2; Finke *et al.* 1992).

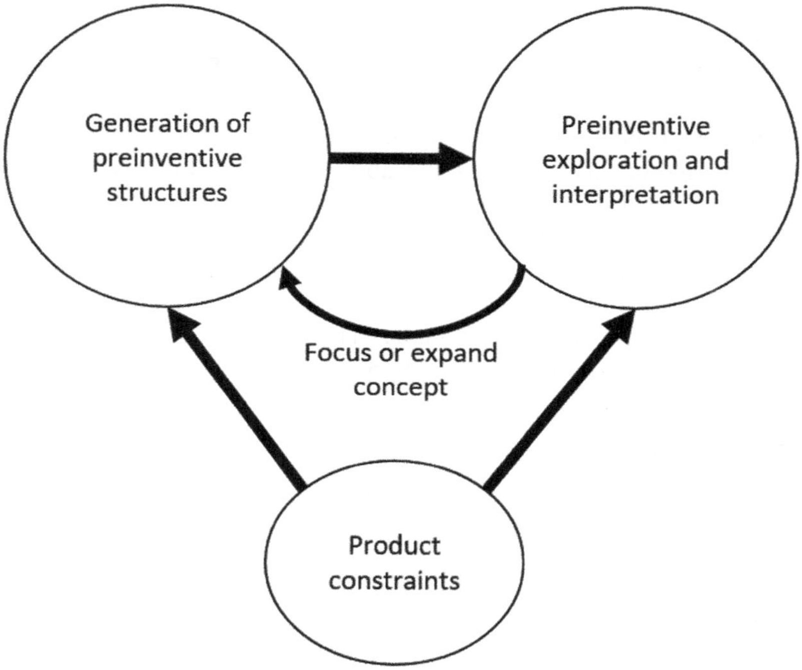

Figure 2.2. *The GENEPLORE model (according to Finke* et al. *1992)*

The generation process consists of the creation of mental representations: the "pre-inventive structures". It consists of generating ideas by making analogies, mental associations and by searching for knowledge related to the problem to be solved. During the exploration process, the pre-inventive structures are evaluated in relation to the problem. This evaluation leads to concept modifications, and so on, until an adequate concept is obtained to answer the problem. Idea generation and exploration are both performed within the constraints of the problem.

2.1.3. *Analogies*

Several authors have also highlighted the importance of analogies in solving creative problems. When the individual is faced with a new problem, he or she will look for a similar problem in his or her memory in order to work on it and then transfer the solutions to the initial problem. Thus, the individual's experience, and therefore the fact that he or she has comparable problems in his or her memory, is of great importance in facilitating the emergence of creative solutions. This facilitation also requires the ability to make the two problems sufficiently abstract to extract the relevant similarities and make the transfers. It is then a matter of creating a common schema for the two situations, which we call the "problem schema" (Holyoak 1985), with a higher level of abstraction and generality than the representations of the two problems taken individually. This process of analogy making is based on three steps (Holyoak 1985):

– *recovery*, memory search and selection of a relevant analogy for the solution to the problem;

– *projection*, the linking of mental representations of the target situation and the situation selected for the analogy;

– *transfer*, the construction of a solution to the target problem based on the solution identified in the analogous situation.

Creative thinking is the ability to find original solutions to a problem. It is not a question of solving a problem by finding a logical solution, but of finding a solution by association, by analogy. It is not a question of providing a ready-made answer previously learned, nor of "calculating" the relevant solution, but of searching for analogous problems in order to extract knowledge and rules transferable to the target problem. This process of analogy is at the heart of the creative problem-solving activity.

Casakin (2004) distinguishes different categorizations of analogies. First, analogies can be surface or structural. *Surface analogies* correspond to superficial or easily accessible concepts. They are assumed to be easy to generate under normal circumstances.

Structural analogies involve a higher level of relationships based on deeper properties of a known situation.

Analogies can also be intra or inter-domain. *Intra-domain analogies* refer to cases in which the target situation and the known situation belong to similar domains. This facilitates the analogical process and leads rather to surface similarities. *Inter-domain analogies*, on the other hand, refer to cases in which the target situation and the known situation belong to very different domains of knowledge. Their links then correspond to structural analogies.

For example, say the problem situation I need to solve is that school children's backpacks are heavy and this causes health problems. An intra-domain analogy might be to relate this to the fact that tents were heavy for hikers/campers to carry and this was detrimental to the hiking activity. To solve this problem, designers developed different tents based on lighter materials and designed to have less structural materials. If we transfer this solution to the backpack, it implies rethinking the structure of the bag in order to reduce the amount of the heaviest materials and to choose lighter materials. Another possible transfer is to lighten the contents of the bag, replacing books with a digital reader for example. In the first case, the analogy is a surface one since the same solution is applied very directly, whereas in the second case, it is a slightly deeper analogy since we go from "choosing lighter materials" to "replacing books with a digital device". Another intra-domain analogy might be to consider the situation in which the schoolboy walks his large dog, but without difficulty despite its weight: he does not need to carry the dog because it has been trained to follow its young master. The transfer, depending on the depth of the analogy, would correspond, for example, to imagining a moving drone trained to follow the child. An inter-domain analogy could be made with some computer models whose weight and size decrease while the number of their functions and possibilities continues to increase due to the fact that, with the Internet, they can access content in great quantity, and also have remote computing power. A transfer here would be to consider that if the child works online with a machine at home and another at school, he does not need to carry anything anymore.

2.2. The factors of individual creativity

2.2.1. *The individual creativity model*

The creativity process described by Amabile (1988) is both stepwise and iterative. The stages are the presentation of the task, the preparation (collection of information), the generation of ideas, the validation with regard to the criteria of the task and the evaluation of the results leading either to a new cycle or to the end of the process. However, Amabile's work has two specific features: the linking of determining factors for the different stages and the linking of these factors with organizational components.

The links between the identified factors and the stages of the process are shown in Figure 2.3. The first step, *the presentation of the task*, is related to the individual's intrinsic motivation. This is explained by the fact that, generally, the cases in which intrinsic motivation is strong are also those in which the presentation of the problem will be done by the individual himself or herself. Conversely, when the problem is presented by an external source, it often means that the problem does not directly concern or preoccupy the individual who is then at a lower level of intrinsic motivation. The *preparation* stage consists of activating or acquiring the knowledge that is useful for answering the problem posed. This can include the knowledge of algorithms to answer the type of problem posed. A low level of knowledge in this case will oblige the individual to spend a lot of time learning the necessary notions. Conversely, a good level of knowledge implies a saving of time for this stage. Amabile (1988) points out that too much knowledge in this context cannot be negative in itself, but that too many algorithms in memory, in the sense of memorized procedures to answer given problems, can have a negative influence on the preparation phase. The *idea generation* stage and in particular the originality of the generated ideas will be influenced by the intrinsic motivation as well as by the creative thinking skills. The *validation of ideas* with respect to the criteria of the task is based on the skills in the task domain.

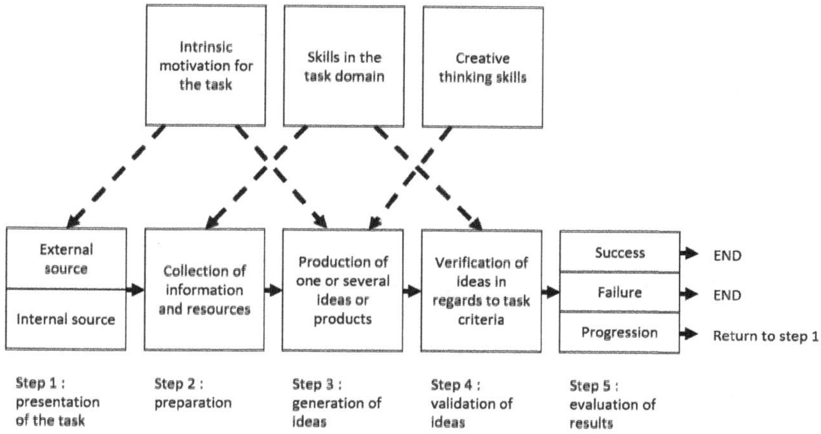

Figure 2.3. *Model of individual creativity (inspired by Amabile 1988)*

2.2.2. *Investment theory*

According to the investment theory (Sternberg 2006), creativity requires the conjunction of six different types of resources: intelligence, knowledge, cognitive styles, personality, motivation and environment.

Intelligence in this context actually refers to three specific intellectual abilities: the ability to summarize problems and redefine them in an original way, the analytical ability to recognize an interesting idea among a set of ideas, and the ability to know how to persuade other people of the value of an idea. Sternberg (2006) states that these three skills must be present together to be effective. For example, strong analytical ability alone leads to critical thinking, but not necessarily to creative thinking.

A certain level of *knowledge* about the field in question is essential for creativity. One cannot imagine making progress in a field that one is totally ignorant of. On the other hand, in some cases, expertise can lead one to remain fixed on a technical vision of the problem which can prevent disruptive ideas from emerging. The novice who is not encumbered by detailed knowledge of the field can bring a "fresh look" without being disturbed by departing from the standards.

Cognitive styles refer to the way in which the individual's abilities are preferentially used. Overall, the "legislative" cognitive style, that is, the tendency to prefer to create one's own rules, is more conducive to creativity than other cognitive styles, such as the "executive" style, i.e. the tendency to prefer to follow already established rules. It is important to differentiate between cognitive styles, which are preferences in terms of functioning, and skills.

Certain *personality* traits are positively correlated with creativity, such as openness to novelty, perseverance and risk-taking. Stenberg (2006) underlines that, globally, the personality profile that is conducive to creativity is the individual who will "buy low and sell high", that is, who will easily take risks, even against the opinions of the majority.

Motivation leads the individual to maintain his or her attention focused on the task. Intrinsic motivation is particularly identified as essential to creativity (Amabile 1983).

The environment can be more or less favorable to creativity, whether it is physical, technical or social.

In some cases, too low a level on one of the six factors can be a very significant obstacle, even blocking creativity. For example, a low level of knowledge can prevent creative activity. In other cases, there may be a form of compensation between different factors, such as motivation, which may counterbalance a personality that is not very conducive to creativity.

2.3. Creativity and personality

Human personality has been studied for decades by psychology. In the sense of this discipline, the notion of personality refers to what underlies the relative stability of individuals' behavior, thoughts and emotions (Funder 2001). Classically, a distinction is made between temperament, which is the innate component of personality, and character, which is the component acquired through socialization experiences. Personality has an influence not only on the behaviors, but also on the thoughts and affects (moods and emotions) of individuals.

2.3.1. *The Myers Briggs Type Indicator*

Scientific descriptions of personality variability first existed in the form of categorical models, before the appearance of dimensional models. Categorical models consider that there are a number of personality types (categories) into which the population falls. The advantage of categorical approaches of this type is that they allow us to clearly qualify individuals so that we can eventually use this information in the way we conduct creativity workshops.

The famous Myers Briggs Type Indicator (MBTI; Myers *et al.* 1985) is widely used in management training. The logic of the test is to position individuals in one of the two boxes of each of the four evaluation points: orientation (introverted or extroverted), perception (intuitive or sensory), judgment (thinking or feeling) and style (perceptive or judgmental). This leads to 16 possible combinations that constitute as many personality types. The validity of the test is questionable in some respects, but it does show a certain consistency in relation to professional activities, since it is known, for example, that engineers tend to be over-represented in the "sensory", "thinking" and "judgmental" profiles (Durling *et al.* 1996).

In a particularly rich study by Choo *et al.* (2014), participants were assessed using the MBTI. Then, they were led to perform ideation sessions using the following methods of classic brainstorming, the 635 method, C-Sketch and all in individual and group settings. It was found that the C-Sketch method was particularly effective for introverts, which is understandable since this method leads participants to work individually without being allowed to speak. This not only makes introverts feel more comfortable, but also makes them perform better. Moreover, the "sensory" participants performed better than the "intuitive" ones, suggesting that the C-Sketch process of iterative evaluation of ideas is comparable to a form of experimentation. Conversely, overall, extroverted participants tended to be better at group activities. In the same study, the authors performed the same type of analysis based on the evaluation of each participant's preferred hat in the 6-hat method. For reasons specific to the statistical analyses performed, the analysis focused only on the comparison of participants preferring the yellow hat (positive, constructive and optimistic) and those preferring the blue hat (organizing and facilitating). The results suggest that blue hats are more likely to be introverts and yellow hats more likely to be extroverts. Indeed, blue hats are better at C-Sketch while yellow hats are much better at group activities such as brainstorming or mind-mapping.

2.3.2. *The Big Five*

Dimensional models, instead of putting individuals into categories, consider that there are a number of personality traits on which each individual is at a higher or lower level. Thus, the description of a given individual is more complicated because it is not limited to a category, but to a level on a set of dimensions called "personality traits". We make the difference between a trait that refers to a tendency to have a given type of feeling often and the state that corresponds to the feeling at a given moment. For example, "trait" anxiety is the tendency to be anxious often, whereas "state" anxiety means that the individual is currently anxious.

Among the many dimensional models of personality, the one that currently has the most consensus is the "Big Five", also called "O.C.E.A.N", in reference to the first letter of each of the five factors:

– *openness to experience* (tolerance and exploration of the unfamiliar);

– *conscientiousness* (degree of organization, perseverance and motivation in goal-directed behavior. Differentiates meticulous, dependable people from sloppy, careless people);

– *extraversion* (amount and intensity of personal interaction, activity level, need for stimulation and ability to be happy);

– *agreeableness* (quality of interpersonal orientation along a continuum from compassionate to conflicting in thoughts, feelings and actions);

– *neuroticism* (stability vs. emotional instability).

Contrary to popular belief, the variability of personalities in a group is negatively correlated with the effectiveness of that group in an ideation workshop. Simply put, the more similar the personalities in a brainstorming group are, the better their performance (Halfhill *et al.* 2005). This result can be explained by the fact that the most homogeneous groups will see less conflict appearing, which is harmful to the activity. This explanation refers to the notion of "personality clash" (Vaccaro 1988), that is, the idea that the probability of conflicts is proportional to the differences between personalities. Thus, when composing groups or subgroups for creative exercises, it is preferable to compose these groups in such a way as to put together individuals who are similar.

2.3.3. *Constituting a group for ideation*

There is an optimal pattern of personalities in a group for achieving best performance on creative tasks. This pattern corresponds to moderate levels of extraversion, high levels of openness to experience and high levels of conscientiousness (Buchanan 1998). Chamorro-Premuzic and Reichenbacher (2008) conducted the same type of measurement, but with separate assessments for divergent and convergent thinking. They observe that openness to experience and extraversion are positively correlated with divergent thinking performance. They also find that anxiety proneness (neuroticism) is negatively correlated with divergent thinking performance, especially when the environment puts pressure on participants. This last point highlights the importance of creating a safe and relaxing environment and program of activities to create the right climate for divergent creativity, especially if some participants have a tendency to anxiety. Finally, the authors did not identify a significant relationship between personality and convergent thinking performance.

Thus, taking personality into account in the way creativity workshops are designed will involve not only forming rather homogeneous groups to reduce the likelihood of conflict, but also by favoring profiles that are open to experience and extraverted for divergence, while creating a benevolent and reassuring climate if possible. Loud group activities can be used if the group as a whole is composed of extraverts. Most of the time, activities that alternate between individual reflection and sharing of results are preferred as they allow introverts to express themselves.

2.4. The factors of organizational creativity

Individual creativity is the most crucial element in an organization dedicated to innovation, but it is not sufficient in itself. The organizational creativity modeled by Amabile (1988) is shown in Figure 2.4. In the stages of creativity, the influence of individual creativity will be exerted mainly on the idea generation stage. The definition of the project is directly influenced by the organization's leaders and middle management's *motivation to innovate*. In concrete terms, this translates into the existence of a place dedicated to innovation, an orientation toward risk-taking rather than maintaining the *status quo*, a form of pride in the team members and their abilities, and an offensive strategy to take the lead in the future rather than a defensive strategy to protect the organization's position. The *resources and skills of the domain* have an impact on information gathering and idea generation. This refers to having, for example, people with technical knowledge in different departments of the organization to validate the feasibility of innovations or people with knowledge of markets. *Innovation management skills* refer to management styles that have been identified as being more effective in fostering organizational creativity, such as a good balance between constraint and freedom, collaborative and participative management, fair and generous recognition of creative efforts, and open communication, whether top-down, bottom-up or lateral.

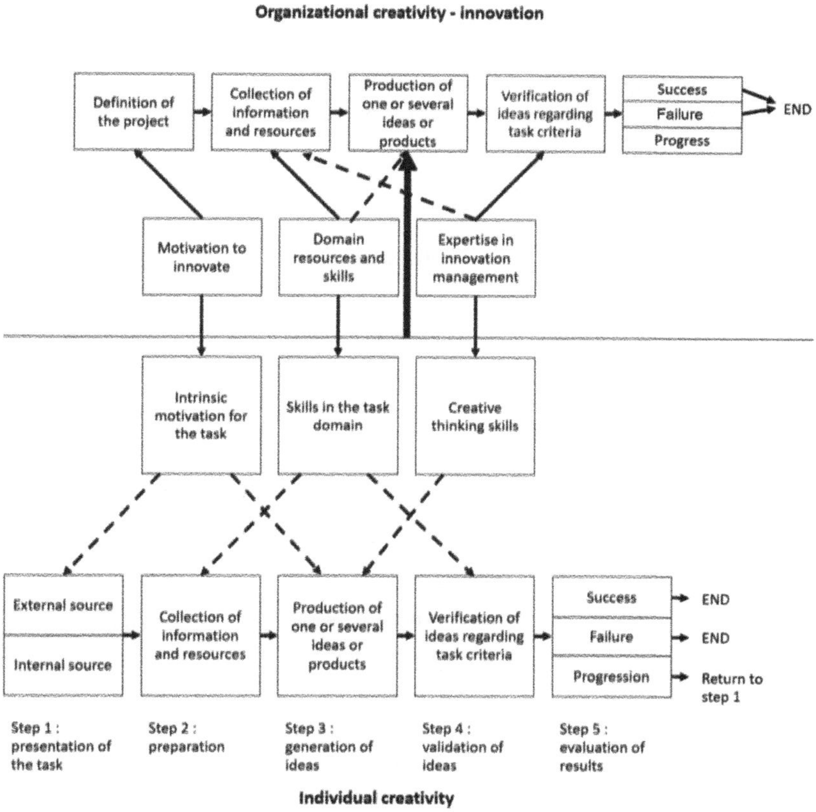

Figure 2.4. *Model of organizational creativity (according to Amabile 1988)*

Csikszentmihalyi (1999) has developed a model of creativity that describes it as being dependent on three elements (see Figure 2.5): the individual, the domain (the individual's culture and knowledge) and the terrain (people with a role in the domain). The individual retrieves information from the domain, that is knowledge associated with the culture under consideration, and will process it according to their characteristics (motivations, background, etc.). From this, they will produce an invention, which will be evaluated by the field, that is, potential users, the industry likely to market the idea, etc. This evaluation may lead to a decision to create a new product. This evaluation can lead to a rejection, to a feedback that will stimulate the individual to improve the concept, or to an acceptance that means that the idea becomes an innovation, now part of the field, or even in some cases of the culture. Thus, the individual's role in this system is to transform domain knowledge by passing through the filter of the field.

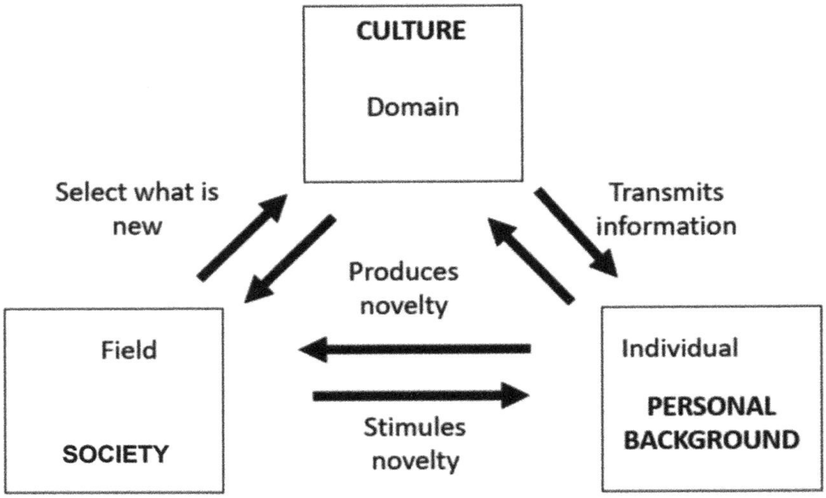

Figure 2.5. *Systemic model of creativity (according to Csikszentmihalyi 1999)*

The specificity of this vision is not the multifactorial character of creativity, but its systemic character. This means that the creative and motivated individual is only one link in the chain, an individual who will play an indispensable but insufficient role. In an organization designed for innovation, we need to ask ourselves how the field is characterized in concrete terms (the company's expertise, the market's knowledge, etc.) and what the field will be (the design office, a community of users, etc.) in order to ensure that each element of the system will be able to fulfill its role.

2.5. Cognitive biases and creativity

Cognitive biases are thinking mechanisms that lead the human brain to draw incorrect conclusions and thus make irrelevant decisions. In order to plan and conduct a creativity workshop, it is essential to understand these biases so that they do not interfere with the functioning of the individuals or the group or, even better, to use them to your advantage.

Figure 2.6 presents a set of cognitive biases that may interfere with the different stages of a creativity workshop. For this representation, we have considered that a creativity workshop was composed of a stage of inspiration or knowledge input on the subject of the workshop, idea generation, idea selection, elaboration/refinement of the chosen idea(s) and a debriefing stage concerning the workshop itself.

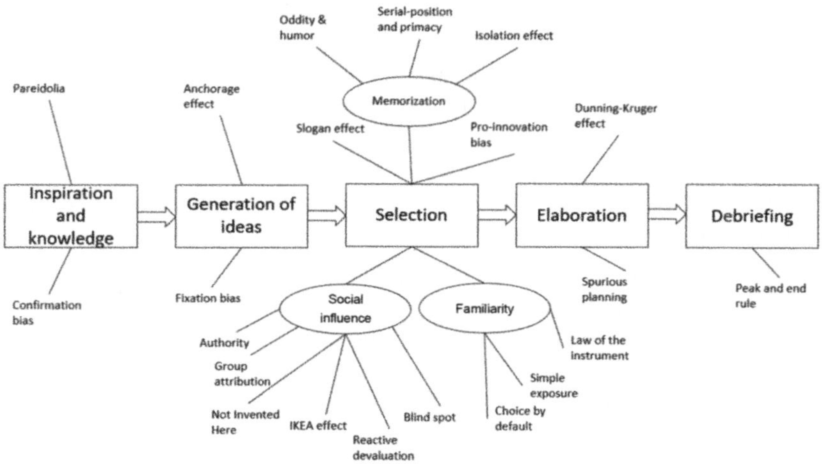

Figure 2.6. *Cognitive biases identified for each step of a creativity workshop*

Pareidolia are perceptual biases that involve recognizing meaningful figures in random shapes, for example, in clouds or in landscapes. The ability to perceive pareidolia is correlated with divergent creativity performance (Diana *et al.* 2020). This phenomenon can be exploited through a rich setting conducive to pareidolia to inspire participants, or the search for pareidolia can be a fun and relevant creative warm-up exercise before a divergence phase. *Confirmation bias* is the tendency to seek out and interpret information in a way that confirms our representations and to ignore information that does not (Oswald and Grosjean 2004). The input of knowledge to participants in a creativity workshop is likely to be filtered and interpreted through this bias, which will impact the creative activity itself (Hallihan *et al.* 2012). This bias is a very present phenomenon in human functioning in general and will therefore actually be found in the different stages of the workshop. For example, if participants are asked to share their favorite ideas in the selection stage, they are likely to have their reasoning biased in ways that confirm their belief. There are several techniques for avoiding confirmation bias. When it is felt that a participant might be irrationally attached to an idea, for example, he or she can be asked to complete an exercise that involves explaining to the group why that idea is bad. In this way, the participant is forced to consider the negative arguments and cannot ignore them.

Anchoring bias is the tendency to focus on a given characteristic of the problem (often the first one indicated) to answer the problem, rather than taking into account all its aspects. This bias is likely to occur during the idea generation phase. To prevent this bias, it is preferable to prepare well the way the problem will be posed to the participants. One possibility is to structure the problem into several bullet points, giving equal visibility to each aspect of the problem, and to leave these bullet points visible in the room during the workshop.

The *fixation bias* is particularly well known and studied for its deleterious effects on idea generation. It is the tendency to always give the same type of answers in a brainstorming session (Kohn 2008). For example, if we ask individuals to name as many alternative uses for an umbrella as possible, there is a good chance that ideas, such as to provide shade, to shelter from the wind and a weapon, will appear, that is, ideas of the type "to protect oneself from something"; these are variations close to the umbrella's original use, which is to protect from rain. Often, the domain in which the fixation takes place corresponds in fact to the most obvious ideas *a priori*. This effect can be reinforced because, when giving the instructions and posing the problem, one is led to give examples of ideas and to look for them among the most obvious ideas. In doing so, the participants are fixed and will tend to give only ideas that are close to the example that has been given. If it is necessary to give examples to make the exercise understandable, then it is better to choose very original examples that are far from the most obvious ideas. For the umbrella task, do not give the example of the parasol, which would accentuate the fixation, but rather indicate that the umbrella handle can be used to measure objects if it is graduated. In this way, it opens up perspectives directly to the participants by showing them that the umbrella is not necessarily used for protection, but that it can be used for many other things, and also that it is possible to add characteristics if necessary. We use a different technique to avoid fixation: we prepare cards in advance representing ideas from very different domains. When participants are generating ideas individually or in subgroups, and when we sense that some of them are running dry or in circles, we simply place a card in front of them representing an idea from a very different domain than what they have been exploring. Participants then become aware of this idea area and this immediately kick-starts the generation of ideas in this new area.

The selection of ideas will notably be influenced by the way in which the ideas and the details concerning them have been memorized. Thus, *memorization biases* are likely to have an influence on this specific stage. We know, for example, that we tend to remember better the items stated at the beginning (primacy effect) and at the end of a series (serial-position effect) because the former may have been easily stored in long-term memory, whereas the latter may have been kept in short-term memory (Lewandowsky and Murdock 1989). Similarly, an idea that is very different from others tends to be remembered better than similar ideas (isolation effect). Finally, humorous or bizarre ideas tend to be remembered better than more conventional ideas (Carlson 2011). Thus, ideas that are funny, strange, original, stated at the beginning or at the end are remembered better than others when these criteria are not relevant to the task. To mitigate the effect of these biases, it is preferable to begin the selection stage with a presentation of the set of ideas, in an order different from the one in which they were generated, going slowly enough so that each idea can be understood and remembered, and without pressing on the possible unusualness of some ideas.

The selection of ideas is also subject to a number of biases related to the various phenomena of *social influence*. Thus, participants tend to follow the choices of other participants when they have no real preference (Fleury *et al.* 2020a). This stems from what psychosociologists call the social evidence effect, that is, the fact that when we are presented with several choices, seeing that other people have made a given choice, gives us the impression that this choice would be better than the others. This bias is accentuated not only by the authority effect, which consists of copying the choices of individuals we consider competent on the subject, but also by authority in the sense of hierarchy (Keum and See 2017). In many situations, social proof and following authority can be considered relevant behavior. The problem in this case is that it will tend to exaggerate the impression of consensus and lead to participants eventually having to work on ideas that were not necessarily their favorites. A number of biases are also based broadly on a preference for what comes from one's self or group and a distrust of what comes from others or other groups. Group attribution bias describes the tendency to think that the characteristics of one member of a group reflect the characteristics of the group as a whole. "Not Invented Here" consists of an aversion to what has not been invented by one's own group (Antons and Piller 2015). Reactive devaluation is the tendency to devalue ideas that come from people presented as adversaries (Reitzig and Sorenson 2013). Relative to this point, there is a temptation to induce competition in idea generation to make it more playful and provide motivation, and this is likely to be effective in getting participants to generate more ideas. However, one should be careful with this practice as it may trigger reactive devaluation during the idea selection stage. Finally, the IKEA effect is the tendency to prefer what one has constructed oneself (Norton *et al.* 2012), that is, one's own ideas in a creative workshop. These different social effects can be neutralized by making sure that participants do not see which person generated each idea. This also implies that when subgroups are conducted, participants should not have to select ideas generated by the different groups because they will be influenced by group effects. For example, they might only be able to choose from ideas in groups other than their own. Finally, the blind spot bias is the tendency to see oneself as less biased than other participants (Pronin and Kugler 2007). It is this bias that means that simply knowing about cognitive biases is not enough to negate them, as we tend to think that they do not apply to ourselves.

Idea selection is also subject to biases related to the *familiarity of ideas*. The law of the instrument refers to the tendency to overestimate familiar solutions to the detriment of alternative solutions. Thus, we will tend to select ideas that are close to our usual way of working at the expense of other approaches that might be more relevant. The effect of simple exposure is the tendency to have a positive attitude toward what we have been exposed to several times before. It is on this mechanism that parts of the effects of advertisements are based: once in the physical or virtual store, you have, "all things being equal", a tendency to preferentially choose the products that seem the most familiar to you and therefore that you have seen in advertising before. Thus, if an individual has been exposed several times to certain ideas, he or she will tend to prefer them even though this criterion is not necessarily relevant to make them "good" ideas. This can refer, for example, to ideas that have been brought up many times in meetings or in the office and that come back during a creative workshop. Finally, when we have a choice between several solutions, we tend to select the one that is most similar to the default choice. To our knowledge, there is no solution that would truly neutralize these familiarity effects. At most, it is possible to limit these effects by using technological tools that will centralize the representations of the ideas so that the participants do not remain, during the workshop, exposed to certain ideas in particular.

Pro-innovation bias also tends to interfere with the selection stage. This is the tendency to be overly optimistic or prefer an idea simply because it is innovative, while overlooking its weaknesses and limitations. A company needs to innovate to survive and grow, to consolidate or expand its position. It is not about innovating for the sake of it, and innovativeness is an interesting criterion when studying creativity, but it is not specifically an indicator of quality from the company's perspective. One solution may be to get participants to evaluate their ideas through criteria that include not only innovativeness, but also technical feasibility, cost, relevance to the need, acceptability, etc. This way, it is possible to highlight the fact that the innovative character is only one criterion among others.

Idea selection can also be biased by elegant slogan-like wording that can make it attractive because it "sounds good" compared to other ideas that may be better, but more difficult to explain. We know, for example, that we tend to give more credence to an aphorism if it rhymes than if it does not (McGlone and Tofighbakhsh 2000). So beware of shocking, impactful formulas. The use of criteria for evaluating ideas, as mentioned above, helps to mitigate the "slogan" effect by forcing us to evaluate ideas in an analytical way.

The elaboration stage is affected by the *Dunning-Kruger effect*. This refers to the tendency to overestimate one's competence when one is incompetent, and conversely to underestimate one's level of competence when one is at a high level of competence (Kruger and Dunning 1999; Dunning *et al.* 2003). In this stage of development, this effect can lead to poor consideration of technical feasibility constraints or cost or time estimates as the less competent may be led to impose themselves. One way of mitigating the consequences of the Dunning-Kruger effect is to lead the participants to argue and discuss the substance so that the estimates and choices are made in the most rational way possible. Another possibility is, when possible, to take advantage of the specialties of each person designated by their role in the company. In an organization, there are certain individuals identified as having this or that technical expertise and who can thus be designated formally or informally as a reference for this domain.

Specifically regarding estimates of work time to complete an idea (and thus estimates of costs and deadlines), participants tend to be subject to the *spurious planning* bias, that is, underestimating the time needed to complete a task (Sullivan 2018). This bias does not occur when estimating the time to complete a task by another person. Thus, to neutralize this bias, this activity should be facilitated in such a way that participants do not make self-estimates, but always make estimates based on their colleagues, or at the very least, challenge the self-estimate of the relevant colleague if he or she is present.

Finally, the end of the creativity workshops is usually followed by a debriefing on the course of the workshop, the methods used and the participants' feelings. This gives the participants an opportunity to express their point of view directly "on the spot" so that the facilitator can discuss it, and it also allows the facilitator to have useful feedback to improve his or her future sessions. This feedback is subject to the so-called "peak and finish" bias. This refers to the fact that participants, when asked to evaluate the pleasantness of a sequence, tend to take into account only the peak of the experience (the most intense moment) and the end of the experience (Do *et al.* 2008). To take advantage of this effect and make workshops memorable, this bias should be taken into account in how the workshop program is designed and exercises are chosen. In particular, consider what will be the highlight of the workshop in terms of feeling: what will be the moment that is experienced as the most intense? This could be, for example, the presentation of an idea in the form of a skit, as this has a playful and stimulating dimension. It is also important to make sure that the workshop ends with an activity that will leave a positive impression on the participants. If the workshop ends with a tedious convergence exercise, such as filling in a template to specify the constraints of an idea, this may be very relevant in terms of the project's content, but it will also harm the participants' feelings about the workshop.

3

Physical and Virtual Environments and their Influence on Creativity

In every child there is an artist. The problem is how to remain an artist as you grow up.
PABLO PICASSO

3.1. Physical environment of creation

As we have seen in the previous chapters, creativity is multifactorial. In particular, we have seen that the good progress of the creative process stages depends not only on the characteristics of individuals, but also on the organizational characteristics of the company. The third major category of factors capable of influencing the creative process is the physical environment of the individuals engaged in the ideation process (Dul and Ceylan 2011).

The physical environmental support model aims to highlight the different elements of a physical work environment that are likely to have a significant influence on the creative process (see Figure 3.2). *Functional support* is supposed to limit distractions and also increase well-being, productivity and creativity. This refers to the ergonomic qualities of tools and furniture, the quality of lighting (with daylight if possible), the absence of distractions, adequate space and flexible furniture. *Psychosocial support* can improve well-being and reduce stress levels. This includes the management of private spaces in order to deal with possible interferences that could distract the participants, and also the presence of a window nearby or spaces dedicated to playful or relaxing activities. Finally, support in terms of inspiration corresponds to the idea that individuals can be inspired by the environment itself. This means stimulating, varied, flexible settings with interesting shapes and colors, different from traditional, corporate office settings.

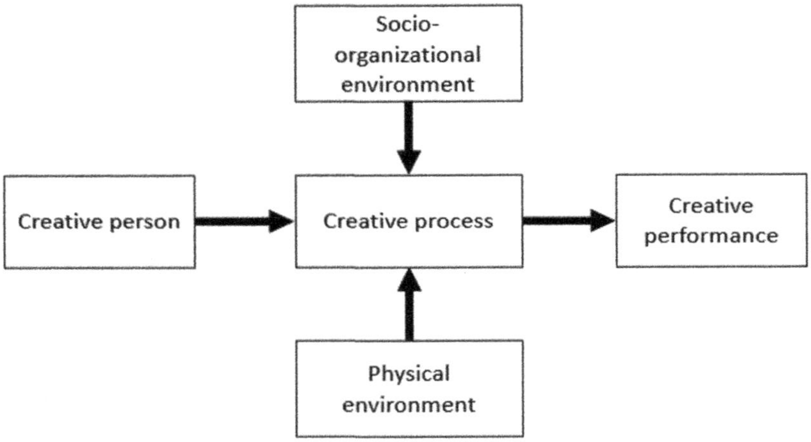

Figure 3.1. *Representation of the types of influences exerted on the creative process and resulting in creative performance (after Dul and Ceylan 2011)*

The purpose of this section is to explore these different crucial points of the design of spaces for creativity in order to describe the main characteristics that the physical environment dedicated to creative workshops should include. To do this, we will first discuss design considerations, then the presence of plants, the choice of colors, lighting, sounds and temperatures and finally the types of postures to be favored.

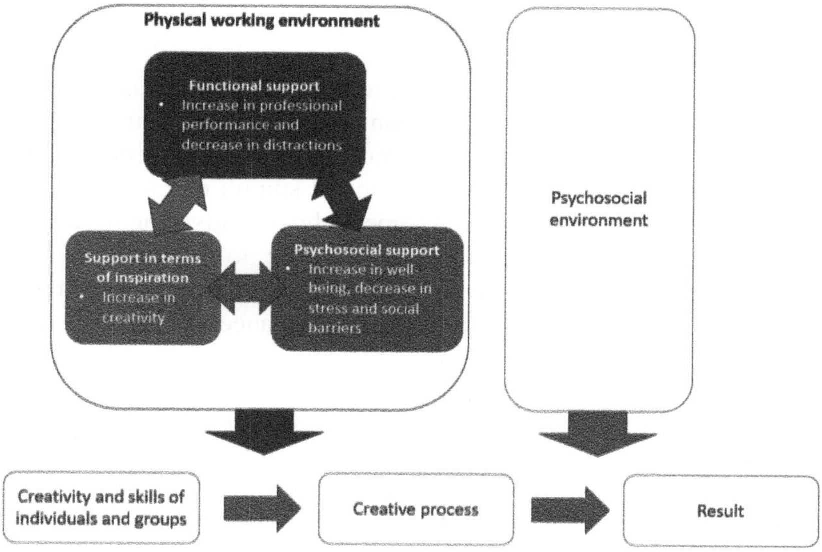

Figure 3.2. *Representation of the "physical environmental support model" (according to Hoff and Öberg 2015). For a color version of this figure, see www.iste.co.uk/fleury/innovation.zip*

3.1.1. *Interference and stimulation*

When thinking about the effects of the physical environment on creativity, it is important to distinguish between elements that are relevant to the task, such as photos that will be used as the basis for a focus group, and irrelevant stimuli (in the sense that they are not related to the task), such as a car passing by the window or people talking loudly in the corridor, which may also have an impact on creativity.

It has long been known, for example, that music with speech or even just people talking will interfere with the comprehension of a cognitive task, provided that the task has a verbal component (Martin *et al.* 1988). Ergonomists know that to capture someone's attention, it is enough to make noise (Escera *et al.* 2003) or to create movement in the peripheral visual field (Johnston *et al.* 1990).

However, these external elements are not necessarily negative; they may even be beneficial. In some cases, external stimuli can trigger new thinking mechanisms for the proposal of new ideas (Jett and George 2003). A rich environment can also increase the quality of the ideas produced (Goldschmidt and Smolkov 2006). Conversely, some studies show deleterious effects of external stimuli on creativity (e.g. Mochi and Madjar 2018), leading some authors to advocate for a clean and simple to grasp environment in order to increase creative performance (Kosmadoudi *et al.* 2013). The idea being that external stimuli are likely to interfere with the performance of creativity tasks (Kasof 1997).

There is a kind of paradox. On the one hand, enriching the environment would potentially have a stimulating or inspiring effect, even unblocking the creative process. On the other hand, it would hinder individuals by consuming part of their mental resources that they cannot allocate to the creative process.

These different elements lead us to consider that the visual richness of the environment, thus the addition of objects, shapes and colors, should not in itself constitute a nuisance for the participants, but could on the contrary bring a form of inspiration. However, it is important to keep the participants as free as possible from interruptions. This means taking a few precautions:

– ensuring that the area is conspicuously reserved and that colleagues are not likely to enter by surprise;

– choosing a place or time when there will be no "random" noise nearby;

– in terms of method, designing the facilitation of the workshops in such a way as not to have to intervene in the groups or speak while the participants are working. Work periods, even very short ones, should be thought of as sacred periods during which participants should be allowed to follow their train of thought.

3.1.2. *Layout*

It is customary to consider that a colorful and flexible environment is conducive to creativity. Thus, rooms dedicated to creativity have bright colors, various and often surprising shapes and furniture (seats and tables) with wheels. So, is it a fashion effect or is there a real effect on creativity?

First of all, the simple fact of having a place dedicated to creativity is interesting, because it enables the establishment of social rules that are different from other places in the company. The classic social rules of corporate life tend to be obstacles to creativity. For example, the social context of the company invites us to be serious, rational, to weigh our words, to think before we speak and to take into account the judgment of others. Taking individuals out of their usual context makes it more possible, with the right facilitation techniques, to let go of the situation that is essential to creativity workshops. The second obvious advantage is that it allows the space to be arranged in such a way as to encourage the creativity of the people in it. Finally, the third advantage is that a dedicated room can have all the necessary material for the workshops.

Indeed, most of the activities conducted in the framework of creativity workshops require specific equipment. This concerns not only basic equipment such as whiteboards, paperboards, Post-its, but also digital equipment allowing information to be shared: a video projector to share instructions or results, and also mobile applications and tablets or smartphones allowing interactive exercises (Klaxoon, Wooclap, etc.). We know for example that electronic brainwriting is very efficient, but requires the right tools (Magadley and Birdi 2009). Of course, we will come back to this point; virtual reality equipment is becoming more and more indispensable to foster creativity in workshops.

Creativity workshops are based on a sequence of different activities, some of which aim to inspire, others to diverge or converge. The constraints concerning these activities are very different in terms of the number of participants per group, the postures and the material needed. This is why the modular character is a central criterion for the design of a room dedicated to creativity. It allows the creation of distinct and evolving zones according to the activities, since it is enough to roll the chairs to create small working groups or conversely an assembly. Mobile partitions, on feet or on wheels, also make it possible to quickly separate or delimit zones. Zoning can also be done in a more subtle way, using mats or distributed lighting to visually indicate independent areas of the room.

A pragmatic aspect to consider is the satisfaction of physiological needs. The participants are human beings who are involved in an activity for several hours, even a whole day. Depending on the duration, it may be essential to have toilets nearby, but also something to drink and eat. It is a good practice to have a "coffee corner" in the creative space and, above all, to indicate at the beginning of the session the presence of these different elements. In the same vein, since participants are likely to stay for several hours, the furniture used should be comfortable to make this moment enjoyable. Today, many companies include relaxation areas in their design to improve the well-being of employees at work. Relaxing spaces are considered favorable for increasing team creativity (Steiner 2006). This favorable character is dependent on the fact that the relaxing space allows individuals to take a mental break from their usual work activities. These relaxing spaces can moreover correspond to activities such as billiards for example, which can be a kind of very effective transitional break before a creative activity, or between several activities (Lee 2016). The choice of furniture type is also important because it will more or less promote social interactions (McCoy and Evans 2002). Composite materials (plastic, laminate, synthetic fibers or steel) are also considered less conducive to creativity than natural materials such as wood, marble or leather for example (McCoy and Evans 2002). Wood seems to be a particularly interesting material for a room dedicated to creativity.

Figure 3.3. *At the Laval Virtual Center, a ping-pong table is available just in front of the Creative Space, ideal for making breaks friendly and for "disconnecting". For a color version of this figure, see www.iste.co.uk/fleury/innovation.zip*

The issue of privacy must also be considered when designing the space for a given workshop. By "privacy" we mean not being visible to other participants. Overall, scientific studies indicate that privacy, that is, the possibility of isolating oneself, has a positive effect on concentration (Stokols *et al.* 2002), which is necessary for certain work stages. Conversely, the fact of seeing each other is an advantage for certain activities (Toker and Gray 2008). The key is to design the space in such a way that participants can easily be isolated or grouped together (Haner 2005). In practical terms, movable partitions or shelves that separate spaces in which participants can divide or group according to the activities can work very well.

It is extremely important to choose a room with at least one window and, if possible, with a view of natural elements (McCoy and Evans 2002). Natural elements and daylight are both factors that support comfort and creativity. Similarly, decorative elements are also conducive to creativity. They actually increase the visual complexity of the environment, making it potentially more inspiring. This can be personal objects on a desk, books, artworks (sculptures, paintings, etc.) and design objects. Increasing the level of visual detail in the environment tends to promote inspiration (McCoy and Evans 2002).

Thus, the creative room must be furnished with comfortable, attractive, modular furniture, made of natural materials. It should be located close to amenities and a coffee corner and equipped with the necessary equipment for creative workshops (Post-its, flip charts, digital devices, video projectors, etc.). The room should have at least one window and decorative elements on the walls and/or on wooden shelves. The layout should have different spaces with dividers to allow participants to group and separate according to the activities.

3.1.3. *Natural elements*

The concept of attention restoration based on the presence of natural elements was developed by Kaplan (attention restoration theory; 1989, 1995). He suggests that mental fatigue can be reduced by looking at natural elements for a few tens of seconds, thus improving concentration. According to the attention restoration theory, exposure to natural environments promotes brain functions that require little mental effort, thus allowing the recovery of attentional capacities.

According to Kaplan, in order to have attention-restoring properties, the natural environment must have the following four characteristics:

– we must feel immersed in the environment, so it is not a simple image, but an environment that surrounds us with a certain consistency;

– it is not the usual environment, it gives the impression of being far away and letting go of daily worries;

– “soft fascinating”, which corresponds to an environment that will both attract the eye without being tiring to look at;

– exposure must be voluntary and consistent with the individual’s current preferences and goals.

The soft fascinating character is the key element, the other three characteristics being only likely to reduce or increase the relaxing effect.

In a study by Lee *et al.* (2015), 150 participants were asked to perform a simple task of pressing keys based on numbers that appeared on the screen. After 5 minutes, participants performed a 40-second break before repeating the same exercise. During these 40 seconds, an image of a building's roof appeared on the screen. For 75 participants, it was a gray building roof, with no vegetation, while for the other 75, the roof was covered with a green meadow with flowers.

Figure 3.4. *The roof without vegetation (left) and with vegetation (right) used for breaks in the experiment by Lee* et al. *(2015). For a color version of this figure, see www.iste.co.uk/fleury/innovation.zip*

The authors found a greater drop in concentration with the gray roof than with the vegetated roof, and also a greater variability in performance with the gray while it remained stable with the vegetated roof. Thus, according to Lee *et al.* (2015), this suggests that in a work situation, it is possible to engage in "green microbreaks" by looking at vegetation through the window, taking a walk outside or even to a lesser extent through a screen saver.

Overall, a huge number of studies have shown that being in a natural environment, or even just looking at natural elements, improves cognitive functioning, including attention and memory (Berto 2005; Berman *et al.* 2008; Berto *et al.* 2010; Raanaas *et al.* 2011), in addition to reducing perceived or physiological stress

(Ulrich 1981; Hartig *et al.* 1991, 1996; Ulrich *et al.* 1991; Van den Berg *et al.* 2003; de Kort *et al.* 2006; Valtchanov *et al.* 2010; Tyrväinen *et al.* 2014). For example, offices with a view of natural features are known to improve job satisfaction and well-being, reduce stress and low mood, and also reduce sick leave compared to offices without natural features (Heerwagen and Orians 1986; Leather *et al.* 1998; Shibata and Suzuki 2004; Bringslimark *et al.* 2007; Kweon *et al.* 2008). Even hospitals with a view of natural landscapes induce in their patients better recovery, less stress and lower pain perception (Ulrich 1984; Lechtzin *et al.* 2010; Beukeboom *et al.* 2012).

Regarding performance on different kinds of creativity tasks, the results clearly point in the same direction. On creative problem-solving tasks, hikers perform better after spending 4 days in nature (Atchley *et al.* 2012). Convergent creativity performance (remote association test) also tends to be higher in participants who have been on a 6-day canoe trip (Ferraro III 2015).

When students move around a campus, they perform better on a divergent creativity task (finding as many alternative uses for a given object as possible) than when they are inside a building (Oppezzo and Schwarz 2014), but no significant difference appears for convergent creativity. In Shibata and Suzuki's (2004) study, female students were better on a creativity task when sitting in a room with an indoor plant than when sitting in the same room with magazines. Moreover, even managers in industry, if they have to judge offices by photos, consider those with plants and windows to be more conducive to creativity (Ceylan *et al.* 2008).

Plambech and Van Den Bosch (2015) surveyed 70 creative professionals of different ages, genders and professions about their relationship with nature and how they felt it stimulated their creativity. The results of this study indicate that, overall, they felt that nature increased their creativity. It tended to make them more curious and flexible in their thinking. Nature also helped to recover the attentional skills needed to analyze and develop ideas. It played a role in the first two stages of the creative process: preparation and incubation. This effect was also manifested when the stimuli evoking nature were sound. The diffusion of sounds such as the wind blowing or birds singing had a positive influence on creativity (Alawad 2012).

In general, the idea is that humans value contact with natural environments and that these environments are conducive to efficient intellectual functioning. The fact that we live more and more in urban environments means that, for many individuals, contact with nature is rarer. This is why creating work environments that allow for contact with nature, even if they are artificial, such as through plant-like forms, is a way to improve the well-being and mental functioning of employees. This way of designing environments that take into account the human desire for nature is called biophilic design.

Several large companies are already applying the principles of bibliophilic design to the design of their work environments. Amazon's famous "Biosphere" in Seattle is a particularly illustrative example, with offices scattered throughout a five-story greenhouse where exotic trees grow.

Thus, exposure to natural environments has many benefits in terms of concentration, well-being and creativity. A room dedicated to creativity should allow this visual and sound exposure. This can be achieved by providing windows to let in daylight and a view of a natural landscape. It can also be done by adding plants inside the room, or even a biophilic inspired design in the choice of shapes and colors.

3.1.4. *Colors, sounds, light and temperature*

In general, the color code of a given room is either made up of warm colors (yellow, orange and red), cold colors (blue, green and purple) or an absence of color (black, white and shades of gray). The question we ask ourselves when we design a physical or virtual space dedicated to creativity is to know if this space should be dressed with warm colors or with cold colors.

It can be said that this subject has been the subject of debate in the scientific community. On the one hand, McCoy and Evans (2002) show that cold colors tend to negatively influence creativity while warm colors have no effect. On the other hand, Ceylan *et al.* (2008) obtain a positive effect of cold colors on creativity and a rather inhibiting effect of warm colors. Other studies lead to the conclusion that both cold and warm colors can have a positive effect on creativity (Dul *et al.* 2011; Dul and Ceylan 2011, 2014).

This apparent contradiction comes from the fact that different colors are favorable to different stages of the creative process (Haner 2005). Thus, warm, stimulating colors would be more conducive to the stages of divergence, whereas cold, soothing colors would be favorable to the concentration necessary for convergence. Moreover, in these two stages, an environment without color (black, white and gray) is harmful to creativity (Hoff and Öberg 2015; Lee 2016).

The scientific data concerning the effects of lighting on creativity follow a pattern relatively similar to those concerning colors. Some studies show that insufficient lighting can inhibit creativity (Alencar and Bruno-Faria 1997; Ceylan *et al.* 2008), while others show, on the contrary, that darkness and dim lighting are conducive to creativity, although it impairs performance on analytical tasks (e.g. Steidle and Werth 2013). On the other hand, exposure to daylight appears to be a positive factor for creativity (Dul and Ceylan 2014; Hoff and Öberg 2015), which can possibly be related to the effects of natural elements discussed above. Professional creatives (from film and video games) interviewed by Hoff and Öberg (2015) consider the need for light to depend on the type of activity they are doing. The main factor mentioned is that this light needs to be controllable and consistent, both for efficiency and for well-being. Daylight is also considered a positive point in terms of performance due to its positive effect on morale.

Regarding the temperature, it should be kept comfortable, but not too hot, or else creativity will be inhibited (Alencar and Bruno-Faria 1997; Martens 2011). It is also best to ensure that there are no bad smells, or even that there is a pleasant smell (Dul *et al.* 2011; Dul and Ceylan 2014).

A noisy environment is generally considered distracting and therefore deleterious to creativity (Stokols *et al.* 2002). Conversely, positive sounds, such as nature sounds (water flow, wind blowing and birds singing) or music can have a positive impact on creativity (Dul and Ceylan 2014). Specifically, listening to upbeat music tends to facilitate divergent creativity tasks (Ritter and Ferguson 2017).

Thus, regarding colors, sounds, light and temperature, your creative space should be composed of a space with warm colors for divergence and another with cool colors for convergence. This forces participants to move around, but as we will see in the next section, this is a good thing! These spaces should have windows that let in natural light and ideally overlook vegetation. The smell should be discreet and pleasant and the environment should be quiet and soundproof. Music can be used sparingly during the divergence phase.

3.1.5. *Creativity, posture and movement*

Many writers and philosophers have discussed the idea that walking facilitates thinking. It is common to observe people who cannot make a phone call without walking back and forth. To explain this phenomenon, it is generally said that walking accelerates the heart rate, thus circulating more blood and oxygen to the muscles and organs, including the brain. Walking is also said to connect the rhythm of our body to our mental state, because we do not make a conscious effort when we walk, which leaves the mind available for creative thinking.

This idea is so widespread that when residents of a city are asked to indicate on a map which places are walkable, and other residents of the same city which places are creative, they usually indicate the same places (Bereitschaft 2018). These walkable and creative places are those that facilitate social interactions and physical activities, for example pedestrian squares with café terraces or public parks. The question of the effects of postures and physical activities on all kinds of intellectual performance has been studied in the field of management and organization of work spaces. Thus, a non-sedentary organization of workspaces, that is, the absence of desks assigned to a particular employee, leads to two main consequences. The first is the decrease of territoriality, leading employees to better appropriate the whole space and to move around more. The second consequence is an increase in the level of physiological arousal promoting intellectual work (Knight and Baer 2014). Open postures (shoulders back, chest upright) are also known to promote creativity compared to closed postures (arms crossed or shoulders forward, chest bent forward), regardless of the comfort level associated with each posture (Andolfi *et al.* 2017). These effects of postures are moreover specific to creativity, since no influence is observed on logic tests, for example (Andolfi *et al.* 2017). Even more than posture itself, the match between posture and emotional state is a lever for improving creative performance (Hao *et al.* 2017). The fact that strong emotions, both positive and negative, improve creative performance has been established for about a decade (De Dreu *et al.* 2008). Performance is even higher when positive emotion is associated with an open posture or when negative emotion is associated with a closed posture (Hao *et al.* 2017).

Figure 3.5. *Example of a playful physical and mental warm-up activity during a day of creativity workshops. The flexible space is set up especially for this exercise and is reconfigured very quickly afterward. The participants are led to get physically and mentally in motion in order to optimize their intellectual functioning during the rest of the workshop. For a color version of this figure, see www.iste.co.uk/fleury/innovation.zip*

The classic posture in office work is a seated, rather closed position. Conversely, virtual reality is conducive to standing use, which not only increases individuals' engagement in the task, their interest and enthusiasm (Finch *et al.* 2017), but also allows for better regulation of stress levels and better allocation of attentional resources (Gilson *et al.* 2017). It gets users moving and active both physically and mentally. It is also often adequate to bring users to a more salient experience due in particular to scale 1 immersion, characterized by intense emotions. Beyond laboratory assessments in very controlled situations mentioned in the previous chapter, which show the effectiveness of virtual reality for sketch-ideas, we can see that the main characteristics linked to the uses of virtual reality allow users to be placed in situations that are conducive to creativity.

Moreover, virtual reality also makes it easy to exploit a specific characteristic of the human brain, which is that we perform better intellectually, more creatively, when we are in motion than when we are stationary. A study conducted in our laboratory shows that when you perform a Guilford divergence task (the so-called alternative uses task, imagining in a limited time a maximum of possible uses of a brick) with a virtual reality headset over your eyes, your creative performance is significantly higher when the virtual environment gives you the impression that you are moving than when it gives you the impression that you are stationary (Fleury *et al.* 2020b). This effect is thought to be based on the fact that the cerebellum plays a central role in both motor functions and visual perceptual processing (Baumann *et al.* 2015) and specifically in motion perception (Nawrot and Rizzo 1995) and visual attention (Brissenden and Somers 2019). The cerebellum is also involved in working memory function (Küper *et al.* 2016). Finally, the cerebellum is involved in various creative tasks (Levy *et al.* 2013). It is particularly so in idea generation tasks, that is, in divergent creativity tasks rather than in convergence tasks. Yet, precisely, our results indicate that the effect of visual motion on creativity works only for a divergence task but not for a convergence task. Thus, virtual reality can easily exploit this effect by designing creativity applications that simulate motion in order to amplify the intellectual functioning of users.

Figure 3.6. *Example of a virtual reality design meeting situation. The user is standing and physically moving throughout the exchange, while the other users are physically at a distance. For a color version of this figure, see www.iste.co.uk/fleury/innovation.zip*

The physical environment must allow for freedom of posture, since the ideal posture is one that corresponds to the individual's emotional state. Different types of seating must therefore be offered, from the footstool to the high chair. The space should also be organized in such a way that the different activities lead to standing up regularly and walking: an effective solution is to slip short breaks into creative exercises, breaks during which participants will move around in an inspiring place, with natural or artistic elements to look at.

Figure 3.7. *The Creative Space used by our team at the Laval Virtual Center was designed to be the ideal place for creative workshops. This is a computer-generated image showing an example of the layout of this space. The previous figure shows the real space. For a color version of this figure, see www.iste.co.uk/fleury/innovation.zip*

The Creative Space used by our team at the Laval Virtual Center has the particularity of having been designed and fitted out especially to optimize the potential of participants in creative workshops. It is a room large enough to perform playful physical exercises (ball games, etc.) and to set up separate spaces if needed. Many different types of furniture are available in a nearby storeroom to create the appropriate layout for each session according to the program designed by the facilitators. The furniture in question is on wheels, including large wooden bleachers to create contact with this natural material. The colors are bright and varied, allowing a specific color code to be chosen for each session or exercise. One side of the room is covered with windows overlooking trees, and plants are added to the interior of the room. A video projector is installed on the ceiling, electrical and network outlets are installed on all walls and a cabinet contains paper, pencils, paperboards, Post-it notes, etc. Finally, since the creativity workshops conducted by our team for companies are often about opportunities related to immersive technologies for the company, we take advantage of the exceptional human and technological ecosystem at the Laval Virtual Center to inject knowledge and inspiration into the workshops not only through technology demonstration sequences (participants have the opportunity to test many immersive applications to learn about them), but also through the intervention of experts who will make brief presentations and/or answer questions from participants. The ability to activate all the levers that promote creativity, which is associated with adequate animation techniques, leads to spectacular results compared to what would be obtained in more traditional conditions.

3.2. Virtual creation environment

Not all companies can put their employees in offices immersed in organically designed plant greenhouses, as Amazon does in Seattle. This power of the natural landscape can be partly exploited by adding plants in the workspaces, but it is especially easy to implement it fully through virtual reality. Changing virtual settings is easy: you can have a creative workshop at the foot of a waterfall or in the middle of a canyon without leaving your desk. Not only does virtual reality make the benefits of the settings and postures we identified above accessible, but the virtual reality tools themselves are becoming more and more accessible. The price of the material has indeed considerably decreased during these last years, so that it is possible today to equip oneself in a basic but significant way, for a few hundred euros. In addition, there are now solutions that can be transported and deployed quickly. We have had the opportunity on several occasions to run creativity workshops in our partners' premises, thus verifying that bringing our virtual reality headsets is no longer restrictive. It now only takes a few minutes to install them on site.

Figure 3.8. *Windows Mixed Reality headset in a carrying case for a virtual reality-based creativity workshop at a partner site. All of the materials needed for the planned session were contained in this single case. For a color version of this figure, see www.iste.co.uk/fleury/innovation.zip*

Virtual reality offers new opportunities to create environments specifically optimized to foster creativity. These environments can also be designed to promote postures and movements that are known to improve creativity.

3.2.1. *Avatars*

If it is possible to modulate the virtual environment to make designers more creative, it is also possible to regulate the characteristics of their avatars. Two main results have been highlighted in the context of virtual reality brainstorming: the effect of embodying a character considered creative and the effect of the avatar's self-similarity, that is, the resemblance of the participant and their avatar.

Regarding the effect of embodying a character deemed creative, Guegan *et al.* (2017) identified that engineering students tended to associate creativity with stereotypes associated with inventors. Yet, engineering students using an inventor avatar generated more ideas during brainstorming than those whose avatar was not an inventor, or those who had no avatar at all (Guegan *et al.* 2016). The visual appearance of an avatar has also an impact on how participants approach a problem. When asked to generate solutions for public transportation problems, participants embodying avatars that resembled commuter transit users generated more solutions that addressed user needs, while those embodying inventors generated more technical solutions (Buisine *et al.* 2016).

de Rooij *et al.* (2017) analyzed this identification effect and the effect of avatar self-similarity on creativity in the same study. Participants were asked to generate ideas by embodying an avatar resembling either an artist, an office worker or themselves. Surprisingly, the results indicated that ideas generated by participants embodying avatars resembling themselves were more creative than those of participants embodying avatars of artists or office workers.

Increasingly, virtual environment applications allow users to compose their own avatars, which in turn allow users to create avatars that look like them, thus exploiting the Proteus effect. The Proteus effect refers to the fact that the visual appearance of an avatar influences the way users think and act in a virtual environment. The effects of avatars on creativity are related to the fact that the Proteus or self-resemblance effect, through the increase in identification, generates positive affect, promoting the originality of the ideas generated (Marinussen and de Rooij 2019).

The likelihood of generating original ideas depends in part on the individual's ability to shift attention between different concepts and to retain these concepts in working memory. This ability is called cognitive flexibility (Baas *et al.* 2008). Increasing cognitive flexibility increases the probability of switching between concepts during ideation (de Rooij *et al.* 2015). Positive affect is thus associated with generating original ideas (Baas *et al.* 2008; de Rooij *et al.* 2017) due to the effect of positive affect on cognitive flexibility (de Rooij *et al.* 2015).

In order to make the most of collective intelligence, it is important to understand the dynamics, particularly the influences, that are at play. In a virtual environment, social influences are largely determined by the visual characteristics of the avatars used. Avatars are projections of users, digital representations. Allowing users to personalize their avatars tends to increase their level of satisfaction (Ratan and Hasler 2014), even though users create avatars that do not necessarily resemble them (Dunn and Guadagno 2012), but rather will experiment with multiple identities or highlight certain aspects of their ideal of themselves (Bessière *et al.* 2007; Messinger *et al.* 2008). Several studies have shown an influence of avatars on users' performance in at least two ways: through their individual appearance and through the social identity cues they display (uniforms, costumes, etc.). The influences of avatar identity cues on behavior are attributed to the Proteus effect (Yee and Bailenson 2007). Avatars can be used to promote group coherence, which helps reduce "loitering" during electronic brainstorming, where some users tend to disengage. By adding badges to avatars that reinforce their group image, it is possible to reduce this disengagement and thus improve group performance (Guegan *et al.* 2017).

Collaborative work using virtual reality headsets has given rise to several experiments within our team. Some of these works have specifically aimed at identifying and defining the effects of visual and behavioral characteristics of avatars on the feeling of presence and the ability to work together efficiently. Different types of avatars have been tested with varying levels of visual (human-like) and behavioral fidelity (realistic eye and mouth movements when speaking). They were tested in pair work situations: the first one consisted of solving a three-dimensional (3D) puzzle with one participant who could see the model and the other one who could manipulate the pieces, forcing them to collaborate to succeed in the task. The second work situation was a virtual version of the "Crash on the moon" negotiation exercise. Participants were face to face and had to provide a common response to this problem consisting of prioritizing objects according to their perceived usefulness in the context described in the exercise instruction. The results of these two studies show that the attractiveness of the avatars is not only a hedonic consideration, but has also an impact on the way the interaction takes place and on the performance of the pair. Indeed, visual and behavioral fidelity is associated with a high level of attractiveness and participants are more likely to look at an attractive avatar (Gorisse *et al.* 2020). However, it seems that looking more at one's interlocutor is associated with a better collaborative performance because it will make the exchanges more fluid thanks to the contribution of non-verbal communication. Thus, indirectly, choosing realistic and therefore attractive avatars tends to improve collaborative work performance in virtual reality.

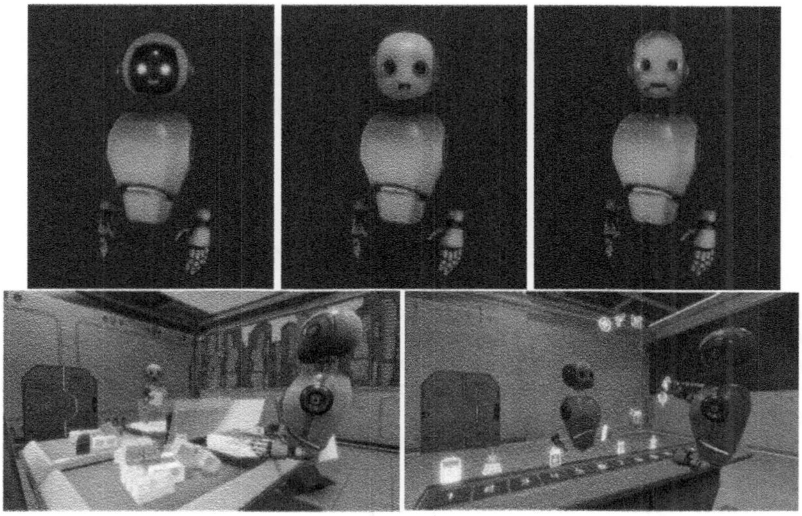

Figure 3.9. *Avatars used in attractiveness and presence studies (top), the level of visual fidelity of avatars increases from left to right; collaborative task situation (bottom left); negotiation task situation (bottom right). For a color version of this figure, see www.iste.co.uk/fleury/innovation.zip*

3.2.2. *Inspiring environments*

We have seen that a virtual environment can simply exploit the effects of natural environments, the effects related to avatars and identification. It is also possible to immerse the users in a virtual environment resulting from a 3D scan and corresponding to the context of use of the future innovation. Immersed ideation in this type of environment saves time, as it reduces the number of sketches and explanations needed to make ideas understood because the elements of the present context do not need to be explained or represented again (Marchand *et al.* 2018).

Figure 3.10. *Virtual environments designed by our team for a furniture ideation session: an inspiring natural environment (left) and an office environment allowing the user to become aware of space and usage constraints (right). For a color version of this figure, see www.iste.co.uk/fleury/innovation.zip*

Virtual reality also makes it possible to immerse users in environments that are relevant and conducive to their creativity, but which simply do not exist in reality. For example, innovations that are thought of in creativity workshops will take shape in the future, in the months to come and potentially for years. Thus, creativity workshops often involve thinking about innovations that will actually take place in the future, in the world as it will be later. For this reason, we have designed an application within our team that allows you to immerse yourself in the future to serve as inspiration for ideation. Several dates have been thought of, from the distant future to the near future, and it is possible to move in the environment in 3D, in multi-user, and to imagine in this context the innovations, even to draw them in 3D.

Figure 3.11. *Environments designed to immerse participants in a city of the future to imagine innovations in that context. Participants can collaboratively move around the city or an apartment and draw the innovations they imagine together. For a color version of this figure, see www.iste.co.uk/fleury/innovation.zip*

4

User-Centered Innovation Methods: Design Thinking, Double Diamond, Lean UX and Time to Concept

Knowing how to listen means possessing,
in addition to one's own, the brains of others.
LEONARDO DA VINCI

4.1. Design Thinking

Design Thinking is a user-centered innovation approach developed by Rolf Faste in the 1980s at Stanford University. This approach is structured to take into account, as much as possible, the characteristics, needs and expectations of the potential future users of the innovation being designed. This also means that *the approach is not techno-centric*. In other words, the designer does not start their project using the technologies they master; the designer enters in contact with the users of the service/product to identify needs, without presuppositions about the solutions. This point is far from neutral: it implies that the *starting point* of a Design Thinking approach is neither an identified need nor a technological opportunity, but a *desire to innovate*. A typical situation in which Design Thinking is particularly relevant is when a company wants to improve an existing service or product.

The Design School of Stanford University defines the Design Thinking process in five successive steps. It includes occasional loops and backtracking.

The purpose of *empathy* is to identify all the needs of users with regard to the task in hand. This involves an analysis of the context and constraints based on various specific methods such as interviews or shadowing[1].

The *definition* consists of choosing an angle for the project, that is, selecting the need (among those identified in the previous step) that the company will address. To do this, the creation of *personas* and experience maps allows for identifying the *most important points* to be addressed to improve the user experience. At this stage, the question of technical feasibility begins to be taken into account, albeit superficially, so as not to choose a need that cannot be addressed.

Ideation is the step that will lead to the implementation of the different creativity techniques in order to define the technical solution that will allow to answer the need defined during the previous step.

Prototyping is the first step in the technical realization of the project. It consists of creating the first representations, more or less realistic and more or less functional of the product or service.

Testing consists of confronting future users with the prototype in order to identify usability problems and to evaluate the adequacy of the need. The prototyping and testing stages are by nature inclined to be articulated in an iterative way: each test leads to corrections on the prototype.

In reality, these steps are theoretical. The start of a project in a company often has at its origin an identified, even defined need. Thus, the project frequently starts at the ideation stage, that is, the reflection on solutions to meet the defined need. The only cases in which a

1 Technique consisting of following users "like their shadow" in order to understand their activity and the associated constraints.

Design Thinking project really starts with empathy is when a company wants to innovate, for example, to improve a service.

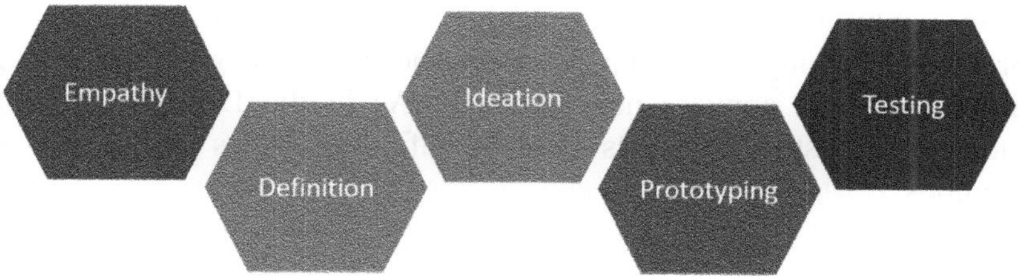

Figure 4.1. *The five steps of Design Thinking by Stanford University. For a color version of this figure, see www.iste.co.uk/fleury/innovation.zip*

The fact that design choices are guided by the needs expressed by future users could lead to the fear that Design Thinking can lead only to incremental innovations, never to disruptive innovations. In reality, it should be noted that on the contrary, the designer can allow himself or herself to integrate his or her most daring and risky ideas because the iterative nature of the process means that they will automatically be ejected from the project if they do not prove to be relevant. It is therefore both a user-centered method and a method that allows for a certain amount of audacity due to its iterative nature.

Iterations can concern all stages, including sometimes stages that are not directly successive in the model. The most frequent iteration inherent to the approach is the prototyping/testing loop. However, the tests can also lead to redefining the problem or to collecting other needs, or even to generating other ideas for the project and thus iterating on all the steps.

We can consider that this five-step model can be thought of in two main parts: the stage concerning the needs and the stage concerning the technical solutions to meet the needs. The first stage aims to lead to a well-defined need (empathy + definition) and the second to a designed and validated solution (ideation + prototyping + testing). This division into two major stages has been proposed under the name Double Diamond.

4.2. The Double Diamond

The Double Diamond is an innovative project management method proposed by the UK Design Council. This model describes the design process as being made up of four successive stages, alternating divergence and convergence activities. As in the Design Thinking model, each stage presents both specific objectives and a set of methods.

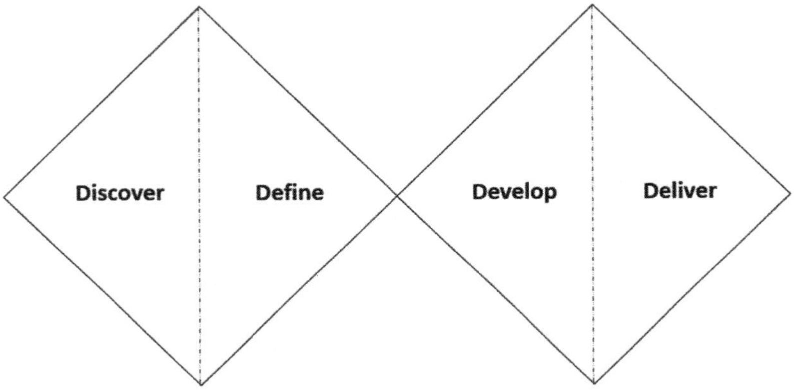

Figure 4.2. *The UK Design Council's Double Diamond model*

The first step is to define the problem or need to be addressed. For this, the methods used are primary research (observation of uses, interviews, etc.), secondary research (state of the art), and also collective reflection techniques such as brainstorming or World Café, for example. The second step aims to define the project. It consists of analyzing and summarizing the results collected during the first step and elaborating a vision of the project, that is, the specifications, the objectives sought and the value created. The third step consists of mocking up the solution and evaluating/improving it in an iterative way through ideation workshops or focus groups. Finally, the fourth step is the realization of a functional prototype allowing technical tests to be performed as well as user tests.

This approach is therefore separated into two "diamonds": the first is focused on the needs and the definition of the project, while the second corresponds to the definition and realization of the technical solution. An important aspect of the double diamond is that it represents with equal size the stages of project definition and technical development. The omission or underestimation of the first diamond is an unfortunately frequent error in innovation projects. In concrete terms, this means that the need is poorly defined or appears to be secondary, even though efforts have already been invested in the design of the solution.

4.3. Lean UX

4.3.1. *Uncertainty linked to innovation*

Innovation does not always imply real uncertainty in terms of customer reaction. If a company innovates by creating a new process that makes it possible to produce at a lower cost (and therefore to lower its prices) or to reduce the weight of a transportable object or to solve a problem raised by customers, we know that the implementation of this innovation and the associated expenses correspond to a creation of value that will generate a form of return for the company. On the other hand, when the innovation concerns usage, then the company evolves in an environment of uncertainty, because nobody can affirm that the new product/service that is developed will be adopted by the public. For example, before the huge success of the *Vinted* app, one could not be sure that many people would adopt this service because it involved:

– buying clothes online (without having tried them on);

– wearing clothes already worn by someone else;

– wearing clothes that have not just come out and are therefore not necessarily the latest in fashion.

These different points were all reasons to doubt that such a service would really work.

4.3.2. *Definition*

Lean UX is a method that aims to deal with these particular cases of innovation in a very uncertain environment. It is an excellent approach for a company that is trying to create a blue ocean. We speak of Lean "UX" because it is an approach centered on the customer experience, but we also speak of "Lean Startup" because startups are the main users of this approach, as they are the ones generally creating new products or services. "Lean" originally comes from "Lean Manufacturing". The Lean philosophy is about removing, as much as possible, the "fat" in the processes, that is, to limit waste or excess as much as possible (working time, material, etc.). In Lean Manufacturing, this implies time calculation methods for each operation, just-in-time organizations with zero inventory, etc. In Lean Startups, it is about avoiding investing a lot of effort and therefore money in the production of features or services that will not be adopted.

4.3.3. *The Lean UX loop*

Figure 4.3 describes the iterative process that constitutes the organization of the project in Lean Startup mode. However, there are some preliminary steps before actually entering this loop. First, you need to identify the problem you want to solve and the corresponding target population. This step can take many different forms and can be conducted in the form of "user research" since it corresponds in fact to the first two steps of the Stanford model of Design Thinking (empathy and definition). The next step is to benchmark existing or nearby solutions and identify possible improvements. This will be done through creativity workshops around existing solutions, as is done in the ideation stage of Design Thinking. It is also possible to use tools like a "value proposition caneva" or to write User Stories to clearly define the value proposition and the envisaged functionalities. From these solution ideas, it is then a matter of defining *hypotheses*. For Vinted, for example, an assumption could be that consumers often have clothes in their closet that are in good condition, but that they no longer want to wear. If this assumption turned out to be completely wrong, the concept would fall apart, or would require serious adjustments. Several hypotheses are thus generated and prioritized.

The goal is to keep only the most essential assumptions for the concept. For example, for Vinted, the hypothesis that potential users would prefer a subscription logic to access additional services is too secondary to be among the first to be processed. Indeed, this hypothesis, if it were to prove false, would not at all call into question the general orientation of the project.

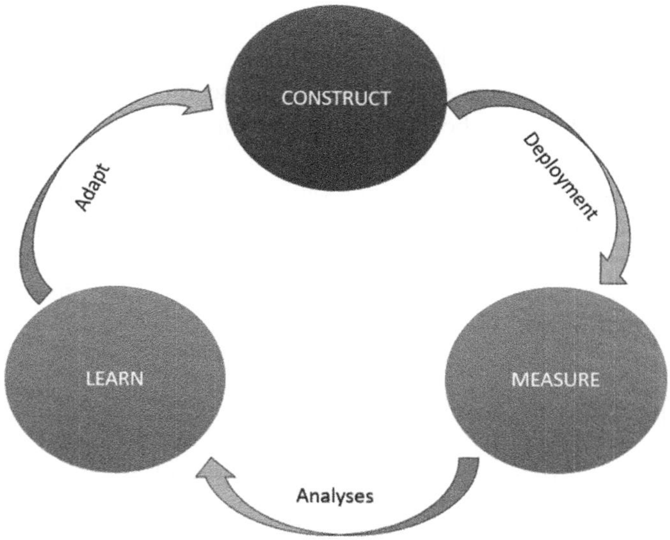

Figure 4.3. *Representation of the "Feedback Loop" or "Lean Startup Cycle". For a color version of this figure, see www.iste.co.uk/fleury/innovation.zip*

When the main hypotheses have been formulated, we enter the loop in the "construction" stage. This involves creating a *Minimum Viable Product* (MVP) that will be used to test the hypotheses. The MVP can be a functional prototype, a model, or even a representation that will be used with the Wizard of Oz technique. The objective of the MVP is to make potential future users understand the value proposition while investing the least amount of effort possible. This MVP is then deployed to potential future users to be tested in order to test the main assumptions. The "Measure" stage consists of collecting as much quantitative and qualitative data as possible about the idea. These data are carefully analyzed, leading to the "Learn" stage. This is the stage where conclusions are drawn about the hypotheses on the basis of the analyzed data. Either a hypothesis is found to be correct, in which case the project can continue and scale up, or it is judged to be wrong, in which case the project or the aspect of the project that depended on the assumption is abandoned, which in the end will be only a moderate waste of resources compared to what it might have been if scaling up had been done directly. In some cases, the hypothesis is not validated but gives rise to a "pivot", that is, a readjustment of the project so that it better corresponds to the data collected in the field. The next step is then the complete realization of the device, the scaling up. The rest of the development can also be done in Lean Startup mode to create new functionalities without taking the risk of losing a lot of time on a functionality that would not correspond to the users' expectations. This project management approach is efficient to evolve in uncertainty while moving forward with controlled expenses to allow for mistakes at a lower cost, a condition particularly conducive to the emergence of radical innovations.

4.4. The Time to Concept method

The Time to Concept method was developed by our team at the *Institut Arts et Métiers de Laval* through a combination of scientific research work conducted in the laboratory and support for industrial companies in the form of ideation workshops, proof of concept development or the MaYAM innovation challenge. Although it can be used in different ways and in various contexts, the Time to Concept method is particularly well suited to cases in which the company wishes to seize an opportunity or avoid risks related to developments in a technological field that is not its own.

4.4.1. *An example of the application of Time to Concept method*

To illustrate the method from a macroscopic point of view, let us take the concrete case of the MaYAM challenge. As previously mentioned, this is a student challenge organized by the *Institut Arts et Métiers de Laval* and which consists of having small groups of students, each accompanied by a lecturer-researcher from the team, work on an innovation concept for the companies participating in the challenge. Our students are specialized in immersive technologies (virtual reality, augmented reality), while the participating companies come from different sectors. They are therefore in a situation where they see a very important development of immersive technologies without being able to evaluate if these evolutions could bring them something or constitute a threat for them. At the same time, they do not have a sufficiently identified interest to really invest in the subject, for example by recruiting an engineer specialized in immersive technologies, but they would not want to miss an opportunity that they would not have perceived and which would give an advantage to their competitors.

How would we organize this challenge if we adopted the Design Thinking model? In this case, we would start by analyzing the company's context, strategy, needs and expectations (empathy stage). In a second step, we would define the need that we will choose to address in the context of the challenge (definition step). In a third step, the students would be presented with a well-identified need defined by the company. Their objective would then be to define a technical solution that would meet this need in the most compliant way possible (ideation stage). Following this, the aim would be to create a proof of concept or a prototype, not necessarily by this group within the framework of the challenge if the workload is too great but rather, for example, with an end-of-studies internship (prototype stage). Finally, a few iterations of user testing/improvement of the prototype would be carried out until a satisfactory result is achieved for the company (test stage). Such an organization based on Design Thinking necessarily leads to a good level of satisfaction of the companies involved if their objective was to achieve an incremental innovation on their service/product. Moreover, this way of doing things in this context does not lead to anything other than incremental innovations while being relatively safe from any risk of radical innovation. The reason is that the company is not familiar with immersive technologies and is not able to imagine the extent of the possibilities associated with this field. It therefore sees its needs in terms of what it thinks is possible.

To illustrate the Time to Concept approach, here is the course of the MaYAM challenge as it actually takes place. Each group of students is given the name of the company and only has access to the information they find on the Internet about it. The students are given no other instructions than to come up with ideas for innovations for this company. A first creativity workshop is then conducted at this stage to come up with three innovation concepts. Then, the students visit the company with an internal point of contact who presents their problems and needs. Based on this visit, the students refine their concepts so that they correspond better to the company's problems. The ideas presented to the company's management are technically viable (because they were developed by experts), daring and surprising (because they were developed without being influenced by the expression of the needs) and relevant (because they were refined in a second phase in light of the needs). It is then the company that chooses which of the ideas presented it would like to see developed. The group can then take the chosen idea further, elaborate it, enrich it and specify it on the technical level. The following steps are the same as in the Design Thinking approach with the realization of a prototype (possibly by an intern recruited by the company convinced by the idea) and the iterations of testing/improvement.

To maximize the chances of producing radical innovations, the Time to Concept approach goes against many design principles by not starting with the need, but with technological expertise. The empathy and convergence stages come second and third to guarantee the adequacy of needs, but the fact of not taking the contextual or needs analysis as the starting point of the approach allows the creativity concerning the technological opportunities to be freed.

4.4.2. *Managing innovation projects in Time to Concept*

The Time to Concept approach is particularly relevant in the context of an open innovation process in which the prescribers will develop the process for a company that does not master the technological domain in question. In this logic, the idea is that the technological experts have a very broad vision of the solution possibilities, but know little about the target company's business and its constraints/needs. Conversely, the company has a very precise vision of what it considers its needs while ignoring the technological possibilities. Alone, the company will tend to imagine simplistic solutions and miss opportunities, while the experts may propose sophisticated but inadequate solutions. The originality of the approach is to solve this problem through the back and forth between the technology experts and the "field experts". The technology experts start, on the basis of a brief survey of the company (and therefore limited knowledge) by conducting a creative divergent workshop aimed at developing several concepts of technological solutions that could be proposed to the company. By doing it this way, they are not blocked in their thinking by the needs identified by the company. This divergence is followed by the empathy stage. In concrete terms, the experts visit the company and discuss its problems. Following this visit, the experts consider that some of their proposals are not adequate, must be discarded or adjusted, and the whole is then presented and discussed with the company. This is the convergence stage. It is a question of presenting the company with innovative ideas for it and its market, and supposed to respond to a need even if it had not been identified by the company itself because it was not aware of the existing technical solutions. It should be noted that this does not preclude meeting the needs previously identified by the company. Convergence consists of elaborating/enriching/clarifying the most relevant concepts by having the experts and the company collaborate. It is also about choosing which concept will lead to a prototype. After that, the partners enter the prototyping/evaluation loop.

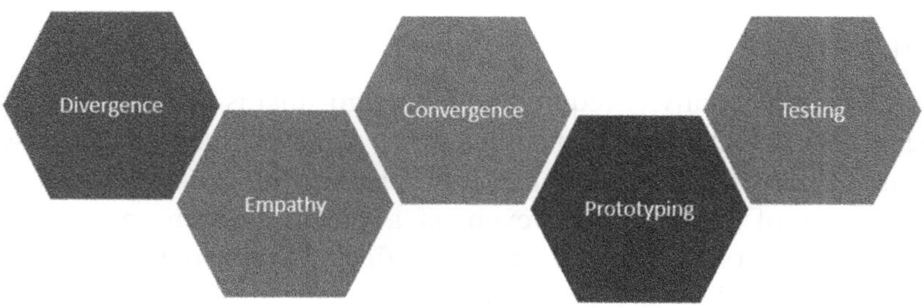

Figure 4.4. *The five steps of the Time to Concept approach represented "Design Thinking style". For a color version of this figure, see www.iste.co.uk/fleury/innovation.zip*

In terms of application cases, we have specified that the Time to Concept approach is particularly appropriate when a company seeks to identify and seize opportunities linked to the development of a technological field that it does not master. It is obviously well suited to the pilot user technique, which makes it possible not only to accentuate the radical nature of the innovations likely to result, but also to open innovation, as we saw with the MaYAM challenge. On the other hand, the Time to Concept method differs from a canonical application of Design Thinking in the sense that it does not start from the users' needs and does not follow the same sequence of steps.

4.4.3. *The six principles of the Time to Concept method*

The second important aspect of the Time to Concept approach is that creative methods are omnipresent in the process, because it is a question of getting people with very different knowledge and language to imagine solutions together. It is therefore a question of creating the optimal conditions for these creative workshops to be as effective as possible, with a particularly high level of requirement on this point due to the fact that these workshops will be more numerous than with other approaches to innovation. The research work carried out at the *Institut Arts et Métiers de Laval*, and also by other researchers, as well as the tests carried out in real-life situations have led us to develop six fundamental principles that allow us to encapsulate the practices and factors that need to be mastered in order to fully optimize creativity workshops.

4.4.3.1. *Play*

Divergent creativity requires a "letting go" that is difficult for some people to achieve and is facilitated by a playful mindset (Bateson *et al.* 2013). The use of games can serve as an ice breaker at the beginning of a session, or even as a creative warm-up. Creative activities can themselves be gamified to promote long-term engagement and focus for participants.

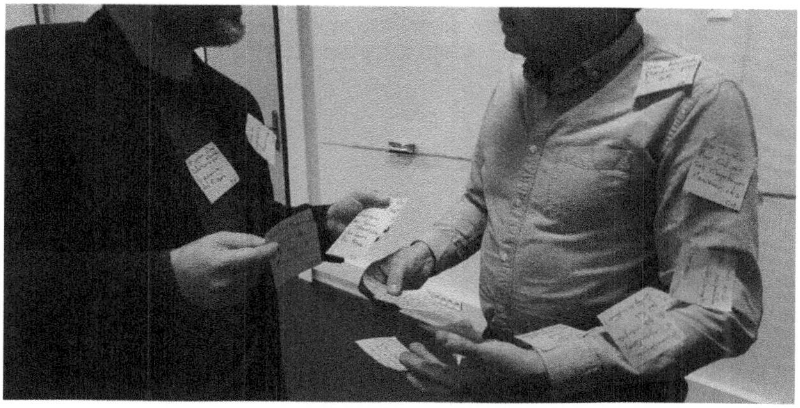

Figure 4.5. *When a Post-it session is conducted right after a collaborative game, participants let go more easily during the divergence, communicate more and are more inventive. For a color version of this figure, see www.iste.co.uk/fleury/innovation.zip*

4.4.3.2. *Moving*

Numerous studies show that we tend to perform better intellectually when we are in motion (Oppezzo and Schwartz 2014). Being on your feet, moving around, are positive factors for creativity. Bodystorming activities allow for this characteristic, as does doing activities more on your feet and taking breaks while moving. It also encourages keeping activities short and changing rooms for each activity.

4.4.3.3. *Inspiring*

Care should always be taken to ensure that workshop participants are able to draw inspiration from several sources. These sources of inspiration can be presentations of benchmarks, prospective studies, interventions by experts, exposure to the ideas of other participants or different inspiration techniques (analogy techniques, etc.) that can be induced by the workshop facilitator.

Figure 4.6. *Examples of inspirations used by our team: a shelf of immersive technologies (left) and a prospective virtual environment that can be configured by the facilitator and allows participants to immerse themselves in a residential neighborhood of the future (right). For a color version of this figure, see www.iste.co.uk/fleury/innovation.zip*

4.4.3.4. *Sketching*

The creative stages are always collective, so it is important to be able to formalize your ideas in order to communicate them. The sketch is a co-creation facilitator (Dorta 2004), it can be realized on paper, in the form of collaborative drawings, in virtual reality, etc.

4.4.3.5. *Customizing*

Several studies show that there are significant correlations between individuals' personality traits and their performance on divergent and convergent creativity tasks (e.g. Sung and Choi 2009; Batey *et al.* 2010). Some people are more comfortable diverging, others converging. Therefore, it is important to use the right techniques to quickly identify the extreme profiles in order to give them roles that match both their interest and their abilities.

4.4.3.6. *Equipping yourself*

A central principle of the Time to Concept approach is taking the time to equip oneself with the best tools and to systematically make the most of new technologies for ideation. This translates into a regular use of Immersive-Storming (the expression we use to designate the immersive version of brainstorming) since it is the best method to activate the six levers previously mentioned. This ideation technique is detailed later in this book.

5

Some Creative Problem-Solving Methods: TRIZ, C-K, CPS, Design Sprint

Great ideas are like air, everyone breathes them, everyone feeds on them.
ALAIN

5.1. The TRIZ method

TRIZ is a method of inventiveness rather than creativity in the sense that it is exclusively about solving technical problems to improve a technology. TRIZ is a Russian acronym that, when translated, means "inventive problem solving theory".

The story began in the 1940s, when a Soviet engineer by the name of Genrich Altshuller and his teams began analyzing hundreds of thousands of patents in order to identify the main principles that guide innovation. He found that most inventions were based on a limited number of geometric, physical or chemical principles. He thus listed 40 general principles at the origin of most inventions. Thus, an engineer faced with a technical problem can apply one of these principles to find an innovative solution.

Problem solving with TRIZ consists, first of all, of translating the problem to be solved in a more abstract way to make it independent of its physical domain by describing it in the form of contradictions. Then comes a generic problem-solving stage. It is a question of identifying the means of solving the contradictions identified. The proposed solutions are also generic, that is, independent of the physical domain of the initial problem. Finally, the third stage consists of making the generic solutions imagined to solve the specific problem concrete.

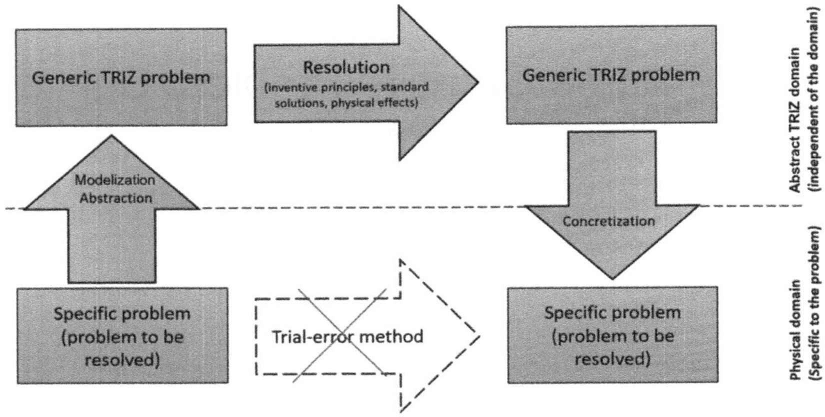

Figure 5.1. *Overall schematic representation of the problem-solving approach with TRIZ. For a color version of this figure, see www.iste.co.uk/fleury/innovation.zip*

To make the contradictions abstract, 39 generic technical parameters leading to the technical systems being defined have been outlined. The abstraction phase then consists of describing the problem in terms of contradictions between generic parameters among the 39. These parameters are, for example, weight, length, surface, volume, energy loss, time loss, etc. A contradiction in the sense of TRIZ refers to the fact that the improvement of a parameter implies the degradation of one or several other parameters. A matrix of technical contradictions then allows us to identify the solution principles that can be implemented to resolve each possible contradiction, which means improving one characteristic without degrading the other. Among the 40 generic principles, we find for example segmentation (dividing an object into independent parts), vibration (making an object vibrate) or porosity (making an object porous).

Finally, the TRIZ method includes a method for combating psychological inertia, that is blockages in the resolution of the problem. The principle is for operators to ask themselves questions about the size of the object, time and costs. For example, "what would happen if the system was tiny?" This method frees up the team by forcing them to reformulate their questions.

5.2. The C-K theory

The C-K theory is a formal model of reasoning followed by the designer when he or she imagines innovative solutions. This model is based on the separation of two "worlds" corresponding to two distinct categories of cognitive objects: concepts and knowledge. When the designer imagines something new, he or she actually generates new concepts. Then, he or she will activate new knowledge by going to see in reality what exists and which resembles the imagined concepts. This new knowledge evokes new concepts and so on. These two actions of generating concepts and activating or acquiring knowledge are complementary and feed each other.

It is in the space of concepts that innovations appear; this is the space of the imagination. The product on which the innovation is going to focus is subject to imaginary modifications in this space, for example by adding a property or removing a constraint. The passage into the space of knowledge makes it possible to transpose these concepts into reality. In order to conceive the object with the imagined modification, it is necessary to acquire knowledge that may be distant from that linked to the initial object. Thanks to this contribution of new knowledge coming from a different domain, the concept can be refined.

The acquisition of knowledge as we go back and forth serves both to improve the concepts and to validate their feasibility. It is thus a question of creating something entirely new and perfectly feasible at the same time.

This model was initially developed by Armand Hatchuel and Benoit Weil (2002, 2009), and was later largely enriched by a whole community of researchers.

5.3. Creative Problem Solving

Creative Problem Solving (CPS) is a method derived from brainstorming developed by Alex Osborn (the inventor of brainstorming) and Sid Parnes. In the classic brainstorming approach, all participants have the same role and the same rules apply to everyone. CPS is unique in that it is based on the fact that different participants will have different roles during the workshop. Each step of the process is thought of as a "breath" consisting of a divergence phase (the inhalation) and a convergence phase (the exhalation). These breaths are done for each of the following eight successive steps:

– *needs* (identifying the goal or challenge to be met);

– *data* (setting the context of the problem and collecting information);

– *objectives* (stating the challenge);

– *ideas* (generating new ideas);

– *criteria* (assessing the appropriateness of solutions);

– *solutions* (choosing the solutions to be retained);

– *adherence* (establishing the schedule and providing the necessary means);

– *development of the action plan* (implementing the solutions).

It is interesting to note that the authors advocate step-by-step breathing, that is, a divergence and a convergence, while not all the steps refer *a priori* to creativity exercises. For example, the step concerning data consists rather of specifying the context and the information useful for problem solving. However, the divergence in this case will aim to collect and note down all the potentially useful information, scanning very widely so as not to run the risk of forgetting anything, and the convergence stage will consist of structuring it to make it usable in the following stages. This breathing logic can be used in various kinds of projects, even if the project does not follow a CPS-type structure.

The participants will divide themselves among three possible roles:

– *the customer*, who will carry the need thanks to a knowledge of the field and a presence throughout the process;

– *the facilitator*, who will develop the application of the method by scripting the workshops and choosing the appropriate convergence techniques according to the constraints and objectives;

– *the resource group*, which will produce the solutions and support the customer through the various stages. The resource group is likely to evolve in size and composition during the different stages. It can be involved in data collection, the formulation of objectives, but especially in the generation of solutions. In some cases, this group corresponds to the people who will have to implement the solutions. In this case, they will participate in the adhesion and development of the action plan.

5.4. Design Sprint

Design Sprint is an approach that aims to apply the different steps of Design Thinking in a short time, usually five days. This approach was developed at Google Venture by Jake Knapp. In the classical approach of Design Thinking, contrary to Lean Startup for example, we usually assume that the product we are working on will be released at the end of the project. While Lean Startup is thought to test concepts and eventually backtrack at a lower cost, Design Thinking is rather thought to iterate on the product in a user-centered way, and to make enough iterations by taking the time it takes so that the product is perfectly adequate with respect to the characteristics and expectations of the users.

Design Thinking is not an agile approach as such, unlike Lean Startup. We could say that Design Sprint consists of doing Design Thinking in an agile way. It is about going through the different design stages very quickly to get to the learning stage as soon as possible, to get real user feedback on the prototype and the concept.

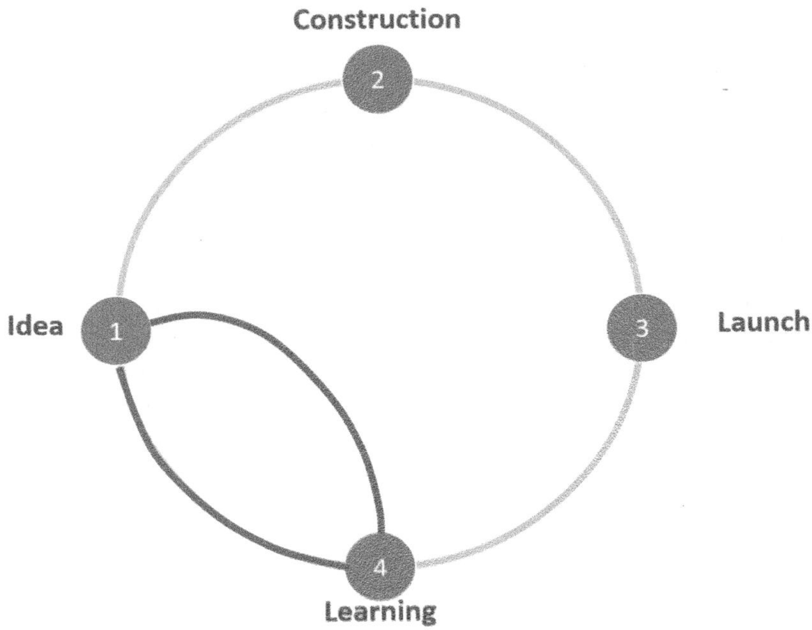

Figure 5.2. *Schematic representation of Design Sprint (from GV.com). For a color version of this figure, see www.iste.co.uk/fleury/innovation.zip*

Why five days? Because it is about applying one step per day, based on the five-step version of IDEO's Design Thinking model.

Understanding: on the first day, the team will need to focus on understanding the target audience, its needs and the associated opportunities and challenges. It is also about defining the success indicators. The deliverable produced at the end of the day can be an experience map.

Outlining: on the second day, participants will work individually to develop one or more solutions to the problems defined the day before.

Deciding: on the third day, participants pool their solution ideas and methodically select those that seem most interesting to develop. The deliverable at the end of the day can be a storyboard describing the idea.

Prototyping: on the fourth day, from the storyboard made the day before, the participants create a prototype that will be used to show the idea to future testers.

Testing: finally, on the fifth day, user tests are conducted as realistically as possible with the prototype and at least five potential future users.

In a classic Design Thinking approach, user tests only lead to recommendations to improve the prototype and continue the project. In the Design Sprint approach, we consider that the very idea that was tested in the prototype can be questioned according to the results of the test. The term "sprint" comes from agile methods and refers to the idea of producing something very quickly to test it and eventually abandon it if it is not relevant. Jake Knapp recommends involving a team of four to seven people in the sprint, including a facilitator called the Sprintmaster, a designer and a decision-maker who will be able to quickly make choices at the end of the sprint. The rest of the team ideally comes from different departments and fields of expertise (marketing, technical, etc.).

5.5. Lateral thinking

The notion of lateral thinking was popularized by Edward de Bono. The general idea is to adopt an original way of thinking about problems in order to identify solutions that would not be "findable" otherwise. It is about thinking "outside of the box". In fact, if a problem has a solution that can be found by thinking linearly, *a priori*, this is not a situation in which fine creativity techniques need to be deployed. It is when this linear thinking is not enough that lateral thinking is the solution!

Edward de Bono suggests triggering lateral thinking by doing what he calls "provocation exercises". These exercises consist of applying transformations to the problem or adding a random dimension to the search for solutions to trigger the inspiration of original solutions.

Thus, during the ideation workshop, participants will use provocations to generate more original ideas. Most of the time (unless the participants are very used to creativity techniques) they will not do them spontaneously. It is up to the facilitator to prepare the exercises, to teach them and to support them. A few examples of exercises to encourage lateral thinking are described below.

A participant selects *a word at random*. This can be done by opening a dictionary on a random page, or with a computer program (e.g. the "random page" button on Wikipedia). The participant next associates this word with the problem in order to generate solution ideas. For example, I came across the word "solitude" in a workshop aimed at imagining the coffee maker of the future. I then think that the coffee maker should be able to make coffee by itself without me having to systematically bring water and coffee to it every time or almost every time. I imagine a coffee maker connected to water (like a washing machine), with a very large supply of coffee and an automatic waste disposal system. If in a creative workshop, a dozen people individually "translated" this word "solitude" (and/or other words) into ideas, the results are likely to be rich.

Participants must *justify and explain why the current object or service is the way it is*. For example: why is my coffee pot shaped like this with a handle? Is it to make pouring easier or to protect from heat? If it protects from heat in another way (with a thermos logic), then the shape can be optimized for the sole purpose of pouring.

Participants *choose something obvious and set out to disprove it*. For example, it may seem obvious that the smell of coffee being made is pleasant and part of the pleasure of coffee for many consumers. In this exercise, for example, participants will explain that in a convivial moment, some people may find the smell of coffee pleasant, but others may well dislike it. By association, this leads to the idea that the coffee maker can be present in a room where several people are gathered and that the noise of the coffee maker can be annoying: a silent coffee maker can be a way of thinking about this.

Another technique is to ask *participants to generate the top two or three most obvious ideas*, and then *not allow them to work on those ideas at first* to force them to think differently.

Lateral thinking can be promoted by *deliberately exaggerating the problem being* worked on. For example, one tries to make sure that the users of the coffee maker know when the coffee is ready without being disturbed by a regular and unpleasant buzzer. It is an exaggeration to say that users forget when they have started the coffee, keep checking to see if it is ready when it is not, and then forget to take it and find it cold later. This leads to the idea that there needs to be visual cues indicating the level of progress (such as a gauge that fills up or even a countdown timer) that flashes to draw attention when it is ready. If the coffee has not been taken 10 minutes after its completion, the coffee maker sends an SMS to the user?

Finally, *the utopia technique* involves asking participants to describe their ideal device without any constraints of price or technical feasibility. For example, maybe the ideal coffee maker is voice-activated, responds to me, recharges itself, makes a different coffee every day, etc.

Overall, the objective of these techniques is to allow participants to take their thinking in different directions. The aim is to avoid vertical linear reasoning which can only lead to the most obvious solution, but not necessarily the most relevant one to solve the problem.

5.6. Synectics

Synectics is a technique conceptualized by William Gordon to facilitate creative problem solving. Etymologically, the word "synectic" refers to the fact of putting together ("syn") elements belonging to different fields ("ectos"). It is in fact about making analogies with more known or better explored domains in order to draw conclusions about the problem.

Temporarily replacing a problem in a familiar domain with an equivalent problem in an unfamiliar domain allows for bolder, less mundane ideas. The idea is to transpose the problem in order to see it from a different angle. In this sense, it is an approach that promotes lateral thinking.

The synectic method is designed to be used with a group of 6–10 people. It is structured in such a way as to lead the participants to make many different analogies in order to see the problem from many possible angles.

Different types of analogies are made by the participants:

– *personal analogy*, which consists of personifying an inanimate element;

– *direct analogy*, which makes links of similarity between different domains;

– *symbolic analogy*, which is based on wordplay, rhymes and poetry;

– *fantastic analogy*, which consists of projecting oneself in the ideal solution (close to the technique of utopia).

Participants are asked to make these different types of analogies in succession and to propose ideas for solutions based on these analogies.

5.7. Detour techniques

To think outside of the box, Guy Aznar suggests using detour techniques. According to him, three successive steps are necessary to come up with original ideas. The first step, *impregnation*, consists of getting the problem into your head. If you start to diverge without having immersed yourself in the problem, you will tend to miss the point by proposing ideas that do not address it. Impregnation is the step that comes right after the problem is formulated. The participants are told what the problem is that we are trying to solve, and then we give them time to become imbued with it, to visualize it. The second step, *distancing*, refers to divergence, to the generation of various ideas without checking their feasibility. Finally, the third stage, *cross-over*, corresponds to the convergence, that is, the selection and validation of ideas.

Detour techniques are used to carry out the removal step. For example, *deformation techniques* consist of deforming the problem or cutting it into sub-problems. This category includes inversion of the problem, SCAMPER or crushing. *Forced encounter techniques* involve choosing elements of the problem and external elements, then deducing ideas from their encounter. For example, bissociation consists of combining two ideas coming from different universes to generate a new idea (the motorcycle and the skis to imagine the snowmobile, for example). *Projections* are techniques that consist of participants projecting themselves into the problem by putting themselves in the place of a person or an object, or by using visual aids (photos, drawings, objects) to stimulate the imagination. *Dreaming* techniques refer to making incongruous connections between elements and putting incompatible elements together to trigger ideas. Techniques related to *graphics* and the *body* refer to the means of expressing ideas through a graphic mode (drawing, making cardboard models, modeling, etc.) or the body (mime, stage play, etc.).

5.8. Discovery matrices

The discovery matrix is a powerful creativity technique conceptualized by Abraham Moles. This technique is also classified by Guy Aznar as a forced encounter technique.

The discovery matrix consists of guiding the idea generation of the workshop participants by making them confront different objects. For example, let us imagine that a furniture designer wants to invent an innovative piece of furniture. Of course, there are many ways to do this, but among them is the discovery matrix. The first step is to list the elements that will be confronted with each other in the matrix. This may be a list of furniture (bed, chair, table, etc.), in which case the exercise will generate ideas that will be combinations of different pieces of furniture, or it may, for example, confront a list of furniture not to itself but to a set of functions or uses. From these two lists, he or she builds a matrix with the furniture on the ordinate and the uses on the abscissa. The creativity exercise will then consist of writing innovative furniture ideas in each of the boxes of the table. For example, at the intersection of "coffee table" and "work on a computer", ideas will be written concerning this furniture and this use, for example a coffee table whose height can be adjusted with a pedal, a coffee table with integrated electrical outlets or a touch table.

The discovery matrix is therefore both easy to implement and an effective way to quickly explore ideas for solutions that would not necessarily have been found spontaneously and that nevertheless remain in a relatively realistic universe, since they are usually hybridized from existing elements.

6

All-Terrain Ideation Techniques: Brainstorming, Brainwriting, Brainsketching, Bodystorming and Immersive-storming

If you want something you've never had, you must be willing to do something you've never done.
PERICLES

6.1. Brainstorming

In the 1940s, the American advertising executive Alex Osborn noticed that many of the meetings in his company, when they were aimed at finding innovative solutions, only resulted in compromises or discussions without achieving any validation. The problem, he said, was that whenever a new idea was shared, meeting participants tended to block it by immediately assessing its feasibility. He then proposed to establish rules that would allow for two distinct steps in the generation of ideas (divergence) and their selection, validation and development (convergence). Brainstorming was thus born. To be able to carry out the first step correctly, he established that the participants must focus on quantity rather than quality, that they are not allowed to judge the ideas, that the eccentric is allowed and even encouraged and that it is advisable to bounce off the ideas of others to generate new ones.

Brainstorming is a method of collective ideation based on the creativity of participants. It is generally used with a group of 8–10 people, although it is possible to brainstorm with three people for example. A brainstorming session aims to collectively come up with a limited number of creative ideas on a given topic. A brainstorming session is typically conducted in the following manner:

– explanation: participants need to understand what method is being used, what the steps are and why these steps are relevant;

– formulation of the problem for which the participants must propose ideas for solutions;

– announcement of the rules: no criticism, open-mindedness, all ideas are good to formulate, bounce off the ideas of others;

– divergence: the participants throw out their ideas and everything is noted down so that the ideas are visible to everyone (to encourage associations), this can be on a board for example, or a paper-board. There are also solutions on tablets projected on a large screen;

– organization: similar ideas are deleted and ideas that seem to belong to the same category are grouped together with the participants. The categories can be given a title;

– selection: participants will indicate the ideas they think are most interesting to bring to fruition.

Group brainstorming allows everyone to find inspiration in the ideas of others. The group thus generates successive associations of ideas that enable going further than this type of individual work.

In order to avoid various deleterious effects of social influences linked to the fact of expressing one's ideas publicly (Fleury *et al.* 2020a), we recommend carrying out a first round of written brainstorming, with the participants individually filling in Post-it notes, which they will then stick to the board.

Sometimes, the behavior of certain participants tends to interfere with the smooth running of a brainstorming session. For example, a participant may insist on defending their ideas and putting them forward, claiming ownership of them, or making their involvement conditional on the fact that the proposals are in line with their initial idea. Conversely, it can also be a participant who seeks to moderate the possible risks of conflict, thereby limiting the expression of varied and contradictory ideas. In such cases, it is the role of the facilitator to reframe participants whose behavior is detrimental to the brainstorming. Reframing must be done in a delicate and proportionate way, by reminding the participants of the rules they have previously approved.

6.2. Brainwriting

Brainwriting is a creativity technique derived from brainstorming, but which has the particularity of being practiced entirely in writing. The principle of brainwriting is that each participant has access to the ideas of the previous participants at each turn to provide opportunities for association of ideas or inspiration. This method retains the main advantage of brainstorming, that is, it encourages the association of ideas, while allowing for a better control of the social influence mechanisms that can degrade the group's performance.

Brainwriting is an improvement of oral brainstorming which suffers from a number of shortcomings highlighted by several studies in recent years. It is known, for example, that participants in a traditional brainstorming session tend to give less original and fewer ideas when they are in a group than when they realize the discrepancy individually (Lamm and Trommsdorff 1973; Furnham and Yazdanpanahi 1995) because they tend, in a group, to inhibit their ideas which they think would not be understood by everyone (Stroebe *et al.* 2010).

The classic brainwriting procedure is as follows: each participant writes an initial idea on their sheet of paper, then passes the paper to the person on the right. Each participant must then add an idea to the sheet of paper they have received, building on the idea of the person on the left. This procedure continues until each sheet has gone through at least one complete round. Finally, each leaf is summarized. One way to facilitate the process is to use Post-it notes, one for each idea, to be added to the circulating sheets.

Since the participants' writings are being circulated, it is important to make it clear that this is not a spelling exercise so that inhibitions on this point do not hinder the productivity of the exercise. It should also be made clear that drawings/sketches are welcome. If a participant does not understand the idea, they should not verbally question the person next to them, otherwise the silence necessary for brainwriting would be broken. Instead, they can send their sheet back with a request for clarification. Finally, the facilitator can regulate the rhythm of the sheet's passage "by feel". They are not obliged to wait until everyone has written down an idea, and it is not a problem if not everyone has done so. They can also decide to do a second round with the same sheets if they think that it could be fruitful.

6.3. Brainsketching

There is a variation of this exercise called "C-Sketch" for "Collaborative Sketching" (Shah *et al.* 2001). This "brainsketching" technique consists of giving a blank piece of paper to each participant. They are then asked to produce three sketches of ideas, each one responding to the problem. After a few minutes, the papers are passed by each participant to the person on their right. They then have time to add modifications or new ideas. The process is repeated until each paper has been passed through all hands. This exercise can be done with groups of three to eight people. Participants should not talk during this exercise. This has the advantage of forcing them to interpret the sketches, as ambiguity can be useful in terms of creativity, but it also allows the more introverted to express themselves as much as the others.

Brainsketching leads to an improvement on average in the quality of the ideas generated compared to brainstorming and also a gain in terms of quantity (Choo *et al.* 2014). However, brainsketching does not particularly improve ideas in terms of variety or originality, and even decreases performance on these aspects when compared to brainstorming done individually (Choo *et al.* 2014).

6.4. Bodystorming

Bodystorming is a kind of body brainstorming, a useful method for empathy work, idea generation and prototyping. Bodystorming is a facilitation technique that allows us to physically experience a situation and draw out new ideas to develop. The purpose of bodystorming is to physically test a situation. It can also involve changing the environment while developing ideas. We bodystorm to generate unexpected ideas, to facilitate empathy and identify pain points, or to consider alternatives to existing solutions. In other words, we can bodystorm at the very beginning of a project to identify needs, midway through to define a solution, or further downstream to test a prototyped solution. Ergonomists could consider bodystorming as a user test of a situation. User testing consists of observing the interactions between a potential future user and a technology in a context that is as realistic as possible in order to identify problems related to usage and to deduce improvements to be made. Bodystorming is a process similar to user testing in its goals and to some extent in its methods, but it focuses more on the interaction with an environment and a situation than with a technology.

As part of a training course for professionals, we conducted a workshop on the experience of traveling by train. It was an empathy approach whose objective was to identify a certain number of needs or pain points of train users during the journey. In the palette of methods used in this training, a bodystorming session was carried out. Without any real requirement of precision, the dimensions of a train car were reproduced with chairs aligned in a more or less realistic way. We carried out this exercise in two stages. In the first stage, the participants could take accessories that corresponded to what they might have in their bag when they take the train. They would then go and set up with their things as they do when they actually travel, and then they would act out the scene by describing their actions aloud. For example, one participant might take a novel out of his or her bag and dive into it while another spoke to another passenger. At one point, a facilitator enters the area wearing a hat and announces that he or she wants to check tickets.

Once this sequence is over, participants will have to repeat the staging, but with a different role. Each participant chooses a role card describing a persona (the one who relies on the hour-long commute to complete their night's sleep, the one who intends to have breakfast during the commute, the student who is studying, the executive who is dealing with his or her emails, etc.) and has to interpret it. With participants who are not used to this kind of approach, it is preferable that the role cards be very detailed and even scripted because the main interest is not in the improvisation but in the fact of realizing the needs by observing and living the scene. That being said, if participants are able to develop some improvisation, the cards can be less scripted and the exercise will be more fun and memorable.

Ideally, it is possible to film the sequences being played. Then, at a later stage, if possible on the same day, participants can watch the video and take notes on what they identify as difficulties or needs. By looking at the whole scene, they will see, for example, that one person is afraid of missing his or her stop because he or she cannot see the names of the stations, or that another is disturbed in his or her studies by passengers who are talking, etc.

It is also interesting that participants give their feelings about what they have played. Indeed, the feeling is sometimes very different from what the behavior might suggest. For example, when the ticket inspector arrives, a character may be courteous and smiling, but actually be embarrassed to have to interrupt his or her reading, get up to pick up his or her bag and search it for his or her ticket.

As mentioned above, bodystorming could also be used to test a solution idea. For example, it would be possible to replay scenes in which something has been changed, for example the ticket inspector passes by, but he or she does not need to disturb the passengers because he or she knows which seat numbers are sold or not. In this example, the scene could show the limits of this idea through the arrangements between passengers to exchange their seats.

For a bodystorming session to be effective, the participants' commitment must be total. Therefore, it is important not only to get them to a high energy level before starting, but also to explain the process to them so that they understand it and adhere to it.

Generally speaking, the more realistically the environment is simulated, the more relevant the exercise is. However, not all contextual elements are necessary depending on your objectives and, in some cases, unnecessary details may even over-focus participants' attention.

6.5. Immersive-storming

We have chosen to call immersive-storming the practice of carrying out the equivalent of brainstorming in virtual reality. This practice deserves a specific name because it is (after brainstorming, brainwriting, bodystorming or challenge-storming, which emphasize the commitment of the participants) a new evolution of practice which is based on principles that increase the performance of creative workshops.

The principle of immersive-storming is to use immersion to boost the generation, selection and elaboration of ideas by using different virtual levers that promote creativity (avatars, inspiring environments or allowing the solution to be tested in virtual reality, immersive drawing and visualization tools) and that are detailed in the following chapters of this book.

Several works show the added value of virtual reality for ideation (e.g. Feeman *et al.* 2018; Yang *et al.* 2018) and notably several research studies conducted by our team (e.g. Fleury *et al.* 2020b; Mille *et al.* 2020).

Virtual reality equipment is becoming less and less expensive and less and less restrictive: elimination of wires, sensors, sometimes even the computer, improved ergonomics and comfort, etc. In parallel, in terms of software, the choice is widening and many tools are more and more adapted to immersive-storming.

We have seen above that brainstorming avoids the inhibiting effects of judgment regarding the generation of ideas by separating in time the stages of divergence and convergence. Brainwriting avoids certain negative effects of social influence that are detrimental to performance (difficulties in speaking in public, influence of other participants, etc.). Bodystorming uses the same mechanisms by exploiting the fact that individuals tend to be more creative when they are physically in motion, active and standing. Finally, challenge-storming exploits the mechanisms of motivation through competition or coopetition. Immersive-storming allows the different approaches to be made compatible in order to add their advantages. The use of virtual reality lends itself particularly well to the fact of standing and moving during the workshops.

Immersive-storming is conceptualized in connection with the Time to Concept approach because the latter is characterized by the principle according to which each step of the innovation process should be based on the use of the most relevant technology for that step according to the type of project. Immersive-storming is naturally a frequent way to conduct creativity workshops when using a Time to Concept approach. However, brainstorming in virtual reality is just as relevant in a project following a Design Thinking or even Creative Problem-Solving approach for example.

7

Immersive Tools for Every Innovative Situation

People don't always remember what you say, or even what you do,
but they always remember how you made them feel.
MAYA ANGELOU

7.1. Design in virtual reality

To enable non-designers to get involved in design projects, new methods are needed. Co-design, when carried out with the right methods and tools, provides equal opportunities for all participants with diverse skills to co-create ideas simultaneously. However, current co-design processes involving these users tend to limit their contributions to the proposal of basic ideas, only through brainstorming. The co-design approach needs to be enhanced by a suitable representation ecosystem that promotes active participation (Dorta *et al.* 2019).

7.1.1. *The natural gesture*

Some areas of design do not lend themselves well to pencil sketching. This is the case, for example, for the design of car lights, which is not limited to the shape of the headlight, but requires visualizing how the light will look when it is on, on the vehicle and with a realistic lighting context. Thus, the only real alternative to real testing is three-dimensional (3D) simulation. For this specific domain, modeling with a game creation engine allows for rapid prototyping of ideas, and virtual reality allows for visualization of these prototypes to test their impact (Ekströmer *et al.* 2019).

Emerging technologies (virtual and augmented reality, artificial intelligence, connected objects, etc.) can provide tools for activities related to the innovation process and more specifically during the creativity phase. It is therefore necessary to adopt a user-centered approach in order to identify the most appropriate tools to support it. This involves studying the human factor in order to understand the mechanisms put in place and the cognitive resources mobilized during the various activities implemented in the innovation process.

When we draw a 3D object on paper, tablet or with a mouse, we actually perform important mental transformations because the correspondence between the gesture and the shape of the object is not direct. In virtual reality, we can draw directly with the gesture corresponding to the shape of the object. We could say that "what you sketch is what you get".

It is customary to consider that in order to be creative, the media used must be simple and uncluttered to avoid distracting the user (Kosmadoudi *et al.* 2013). Also, in an effort to simplify creativity tasks, some recent work has highlighted the potential of virtual reality tools over traditional tools in this area. For example, Yang *et al.* (2018) compared the performance in a creativity task between a "paper/pencil" condition and a "virtual reality" condition. The use of virtual reality in this study allowed the creativity task to be treated as a 1:1 drawing activity, which led to better creativity performance than drawing by hand (Rieuf 2013). Following a similar logic, Feeman *et al.* (2018) compared the use of CAD software with a virtual reality tool-based equivalent. Again, the simplification of interactions resulting from going through the users' natural gestures tended to facilitate creative tasks. Moreover, this idea that natural gestures are beneficial to creativity is commonly accepted (e.g. Nakagawa 2005). By simplifying interactions, cognitive resources are less mobilized for the use of the tool and more available to respond to the creativity task.

7.1.2. *Links with CAD*

Virtual reality CAD software is an environment in which users can interact with and visualize CAD models, as well as use CAD functionality. There are a number of applications that allow users some basic CAD functionality to create relatively simple models. It is also possible to import CAD models in order to visualize them in virtual reality. Indeed, it is difficult for designers to perceive and evaluate the properties of future products if they are not able to appreciate them in a multimodal and 3D way. It is important to allow users to work with models created on other tools or with data from 3D scans. The applications allow users to create models using prefabricated shapes. These shapes can be manipulated, resized and positioned as needed. Once the model is created, it can be exported as a file for use with a 3D printer or for use by another user of any type of CAD software. Importing a CAD model into a virtual environment allows for better visualization. By being able to move around the model, an engineer can identify potential problems in the future manufacturing of the part. In addition, it is possible to design models directly in a virtual environment in traditional CAD software by using a specific virtual reality interface that will make the link between the two worlds. This is the case of Time2Craft, developed within our team. This software works with Solidworks open, and enables realizing immersion models for headsets, by creating forms directly with the controllers. The interest is to benefit from the natural gesture linked to virtual reality while producing content that can be directly used in CAD. This approach is relevant to begin the design phase, after the end of the ideation phase, or to create the first presentation-sketch.

Figure 7.1. *Screenshots of Time2Craft (top and bottom left): simple shapes can be made in a very clean interface, directly in CAD software (bottom right). For a color version of this figure, see www.iste.co.uk/fleury/innovation. zip*

7.1.3. *Comparison of sketching tools*

Tool comparisons for drawing have been the subject of much research in recent years. In a study by Calderon-Hernandez *et al.* (2019), a comparison was made between 2D drawing and immersive 3D modeling in virtual reality to model the same structure. Participants were asked to perform operations that required viewing the models in both conditions. The results indicate that the virtual reality version of the tool allowed for more accuracy in the activity, in the perception of the models and a better memorization of the visualized models.

Lee *et al.* (2019) explored differences in designer cognitions and creativity related to the use of a 2D or virtual reality design environment. The experiment focused on sketching activity, that is, the ideation phase. Ten fashion designers participated. Half of them used Photoshop CS6 with a digital pen while the other half used an immersive 3D drawing tool (Google Tilt Brush). The goal of the participants was to draw a woman's dress in 20 seconds and then in 30 seconds. For this task, the performance was superior with Tilt Brush in terms of creativity. The authors explained that the fact of changing point of view in virtual reality led the participants to evaluate their initial idea and to change their mind. Conversely, the 2D drawing tool led designers to iterate to elaborate their initial idea, rather than to change their idea in a divergent thinking logic.

Yang and Lee (2020) conducted a study focused on identifying the cognitive impact of sketching in virtual reality for the concept generation phase. Here again, the aim was to compare the performance of designers generating concepts by sketching in virtual reality with designers making these sketches with paper/pencil. According to the authors, sketching in virtual reality stimulates visual-spatial cognition that transforms and reconstructs initial ideas to generate new concepts.

Spatial inspection behavior, which consists of changing the point of view by turning around the object in order to observe it in a general or specific way, is considered as a key behavior of the sketching activity in virtual reality. The different experiments show that users perform spatial inspections very frequently during the sketching process. The fact that virtual reality significantly facilitates spatial inspections would be a major reason for the improved performance, as it would induce an extension of ideas in space, an increase in idea transformations and a more holistic approach (Drey *et al.* 2020).

As we mentioned above, the sketches made in the ideation phase are generally made on paper, or in the worst case on a CAD software with a keyboard and a mouse. These two uses have been experimentally compared to a virtual reality equivalent for tasks involving imagining new products. In the study by Yang *et al.* (2018), participants were asked to represent a technological object with the properties of a smartphone that was not a connected watch. In one condition, they had to perform this ideation task in an immersive 3D drawing environment while in the other condition, they had to perform their sketches on paper. The results indicate that the participants were more creative with virtual reality than with paper. According to the authors, the virtual reality tool is conducive to inducing a state of flow in the participants, which is conducive to creativity. In Feeman *et al.*'s (2018) study, participants were asked to design a chair, either in virtual reality or with computer-based CAD software with a keyboard and mouse. Looking at the productions of the different participants, we see that on the computer the modeled chairs are very simple. They often resemble the most minimalist representation of a chair possible, that is, four legs and a straight backrest. It seems that the participants, faced with an unsatisfactory use of the tool, considered that the task was finished as soon as their production resembled a chair. The models produced by the group of participants using virtual reality were more original in their form, and also more complex. It appears that with the immersive tool participants were more engaged in the task, and even when their output looked like a chair, continued to work to add additional elements. Virtual reality sketching is clearly a superior alternative to paper/pencil and CAD software. Adopting an immersive sketching solution is therefore a simple way to increase the speed and quality of the innovation process. Mille *et al.* (2020) shed additional light by comparing paper/pencil, virtual reality sketching, virtual reality modeling and CAD with keyboard/mouse in the same experiment. This comparison involved an idea generation task for improving an existing product. The results indicate that tools that allow freehand sketching are better at promoting fluidity in idea generation. In addition, virtual reality tools were superior to others in terms of user experience and satisfaction.

7.2. Co-design in virtual reality

Virtual reality offers a unique potential for immersive remote collaboration. Virtual tools, especially since the arrival of powerful virtual and augmented reality headsets, can be integrated into a workflow that places the human being at the center of the creative process by simplifying local and remote collaboration.

7.2.1. *Information capture in virtual reality*

From recent studies, we know that virtual reality is more effective in creating new object concepts than pencil and paper (Yang *et al.* 2018) or CAD (Feeman *et al.* 2018) for a single person. However, creativity workshops classically rely on group methods, such as brainstorming. During these, ideas are often kept in written form, whether on Post-it notes, posters or minutes. In virtual reality, this need to take notes remains because it is often necessary to transmit to other people what happened during a creativity workshop and to keep a written record. While virtual reality can improve performance on creative tasks, the written format may still be an inescapable way to communicate ideas to outsiders. In our team, we have identified three complementary solutions for taking notes during meetings in a virtual environment: the drum-like keyboard (virtual keyboard on which one taps as if with sticks on a drum), generic speech-to-text (when I activate a button, it transcribes the words of all the individuals) and individual speech-to-text (when I press a button, it transcribes my words only; Agnès *et al.* 2020).

Figure 7.2. *On the left, the drum-like keyboard, and on the right, the individual text-to-speech microphone, and the collective text-to-speech recording. For a color version of this figure, see www.iste.co.uk/fleury/innovation.zip*

7.2.2. *Asymmetrical collaboration*

Within the framework of the research and development activities conducted by our laboratory, we are obviously very regularly led to recommend the use of virtual reality for ideation, or to use it ourselves in this context. However, creativity activities are often conducted with a large number of participants, a dozen or more. It is then difficult to imagine organizations with each participant using headphones at the same time, for reasons of availability of material (headphones + computers), and also of physical space. Finally, even if it is less and less frequent due to the improvement of headsets and applications, some people tend to be uncomfortable if they stay under headset for a long time. For these reasons, it is essential to think of organizational modes that allow both the inclusion of virtual reality to benefit from its advantages, while taking into account the constraints of equipment and individual sensitivity.

The most obvious solution is to offer asymmetrical collaboration modes, that is, users collaborate, but with different hardware. A given user may be using a headset while the others are on a computer, for example. The development of hardware diversity and interaction modes suggests that asymmetrical collaborations will become more and more frequent in the future. This raises many questions not only in terms of the design of applications that will have to take this constraint into account, but also in terms of working methods.

Designing with users wearing headsets at the same time is only one possibility among others, and in addition to the material constraints it imposes, it is therefore not always the most relevant. During the creativity workshops led by our team, we usually have a large screen or a video-projection allowing the people present to see in real time what is happening in the virtual environment, to comment and to propose ideas, especially to the people using headphones. In some cases, it is also possible for some users to view the productions in augmented reality from a smartphone or a tablet.

Figure 7.3. *Example of a collaborative work situation with one user immersed in a headset while the second user views the environment on a large screen, commenting on the actions of his or her colleague. For a color version of this figure, see www.iste.co.uk/fleury/innovation.zip*

The limits of traditional face-to-face brainstorming have already been mentioned. The methodology itself, which is based on the principle of collective intelligence based on the association of ideas from one person with those of another, has already been criticized. However, a limitation of traditional brainstorming is also linked to its face-to-face nature. Individuals display their real physical appearance while it is known that it is possible to improve the performance of a group with well-chosen avatars. They are present in a room that cannot be reconfigured *ad infinitum*, unlike a virtual environment. It is also difficult to consider certain settings for brainstorming in real life for reasons of feasibility or cost (such as a brainstorming session at the top of a mountain peak), whereas virtual reality allows you to choose exactly the most suitable setting to optimize the session. We would like to add that, currently, an important part of this optimization comes from the fact of applying in virtual reality knowledge from work in a "tangible" context, such as the knowledge that a brainstorming session will be more effective in the middle of nature, which allows virtual reality sessions to be held in natural settings that would not be physically accessible (at the foot of an exotic waterfall, for example). However, the possibilities of virtual reality obviously go far beyond simply reproducing things that work well in real life. There are probably levers that have not yet been identified and that virtual reality will activate.

7.2.3. *Affordances and constraints for immersive-storming*

Fromm *et al.* (2020) published a study in which participants carried out a series of brainstorming sessions in virtual reality using the Vtime XR software. They identified a certain number of points of vigilance which may concern the design of the tool or the choice of scenery or animation. In particular, and contrary to what one might imagine, the affordances are not always positive for the good progress of an immersive-storming session and the constraints are not always negative. It is easier to stay focused on the task than during a face-to-face or on-screen brainstorming, although a very esthetic setting full of details to explore may appear "more interesting" than the task itself, at the risk of seeing participants drop out.

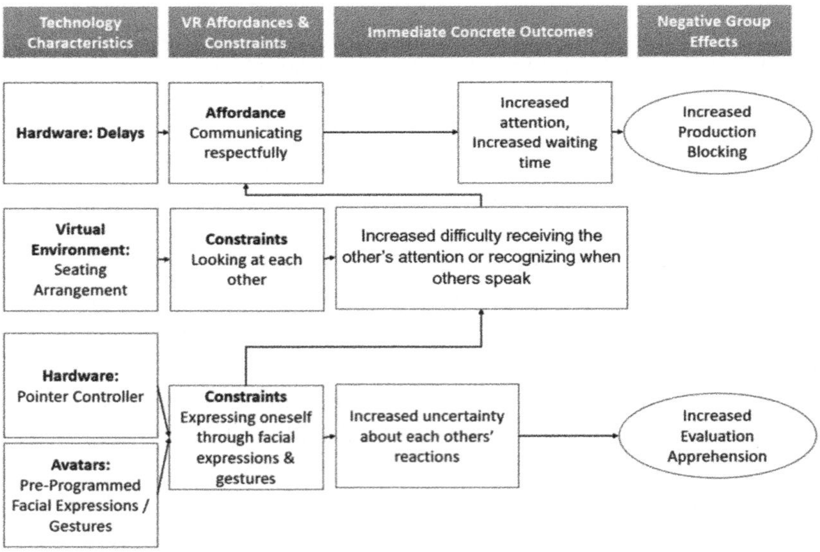

Figure 7.4. *The "Affordance and Constraint Network" (according to Fromm* et al. *2020)*

The "Affordance and Constraint Network" describes the links between the characteristics of the technology used and two known negative effects in brainstorming: production blocking (due to the fact that others are talking) and evaluation apprehension. Thus, one characteristic observed is that there is a delay in the transmission of sound which tends to make the exchanges less fluid. The consequence is that very quickly the participants adopt a more respectful mode of communication by trying to be careful not to cut off their partners' speech. This implies an increase in waiting time and their level of vigilance toward the reactions of other participants, to the detriment of their own train of thought. Having to focus on the form of the exchange ultimately prevents them from focusing on the idea generation itself. This phenomenon is what the authors call "production blocking". To brainstorm in virtual reality, it is therefore very important to ensure that there is no delay in the transmission of sound.

The second negative point highlighted by the authors is related to the management of facial expressions and people's gestures. The expressions are managed automatically by the software to make the avatars more realistic. The consequence of this choice is that these expressions do not necessarily correspond to the real expressions or feelings of the users. This triggers an uncertainty of the participants about the reactions of the other participants and contributes to generating an evaluation apprehension. In addition, it forces them to be more vigilant with regard to the reactions of others, thus accentuating the blockage of production mentioned above.

Thus, according to Fromm *et al.* (2020), virtual reality brainstorming avoids two of the four negative effects classically observed in tangible brainstorming:

– social comparison, which consists of feeling in competition with the other members of the group whereas it is a collaborative production;

– cognitive inertia, which corresponds to the fact of remaining stuck on one's own initial ideas without really finding interest in the ideas of the other participants.

Mitigating these two effects is an important strength of the tool for effective brainstorming. The two negative effects correspond to precise and identified technical points: the bad management of expressions and gestures and the delay of sound transmission which both harm the quality of social interactions. It is therefore important to make sure that these two aspects are well taken care of when choosing a brainstorming application.

7.3. Types of immersive applications for creativity

When we talk about the use of virtual reality for innovation and more specifically for ideation, it actually refers to a whole set of different categories of applications and uses.

First of all, and as has been demonstrated on the basis of numerous scientific research studies already mentioned, virtual reality offers an important potential for ideation in the form of drawings or sketches. There are freehand drawing tools in which the user makes sketches in 3D. Some tools work more with a sculpting logic in the sense that the user will have the sensation of adding or removing material. Finally, the third major type of tool consists of creating 3D shapes from deformable primitives. These different tools can be used individually or collectively, but also asymmetrically (one user using a headset, another in front of a screen, for example) and asynchronously (the users do not connect at the same time, but continue the same work). The immersive sketching tool can really take place in a brainstorming session in which the sketching is fast, the ideas are quickly drawn freehand and selected in a second time. This solution has the advantage of immersing users in an environment relevant to the question they have to solve.

Immersive technologies are also used for ideation through visualization tools. It is not uncommon for brainstorming sessions in companies to focus on technical problems to be solved. The fact of visualizing in immersion the elements can constitute precious help because it allows for realizing the real proportions more successfully. For example, making design choices by moving physically in a virtual version of the place facilitates decision making considerably.

Figure 7.5. *Augmented reality visualization of a 3D mechanical part with an animation showing the direction of flow in the part. For a color version of this figure, see www.iste.co.uk/fleury/innovation.zip*

Immersive meeting tools can also be used for ideation activities, especially when the participants are working remotely. These tools are by nature more adapted than classic videoconferencing tools for creative activities because they can be used standing up, in an active posture, or even in motion, which is an important prerequisite to increase creativity. Then, it is important to select the right tool according to the useful functionalities of the workshop and the type of animation desired. For example, some tools allow you to import and manipulate 3D parts, images to make a presentation, to make drawings or to post Post-it notes.

Figure 7.6. *Virtual reality meeting situation in our team with presentation of results graphs: instead of displaying a slide show on a screen, the graphs are spread out on the walls of the virtual room. Thus, during the presentation, the facilitator and his colleagues move around the environment, viewing each graph as they would move from painting to painting in a museum. For a color version of this figure, see www.iste.co.uk/fleury/innovation.zip*

For ideation sessions on specific subjects, it is sometimes possible to find applications with very precise functionalities. For example, a creative work around the shape of future car lights or office lamps could gain considerably in efficiency if it is carried out in immersion in a virtual environment simulating in a realistic way the light in the environment according to the modifications of forms carried out. In the same way, if the question concerns the design of a place, a solution allowing to scan the place in question, to cut directly in the point cloud and to move the cut objects saves a lot of time by “testing” them directly in immersion.

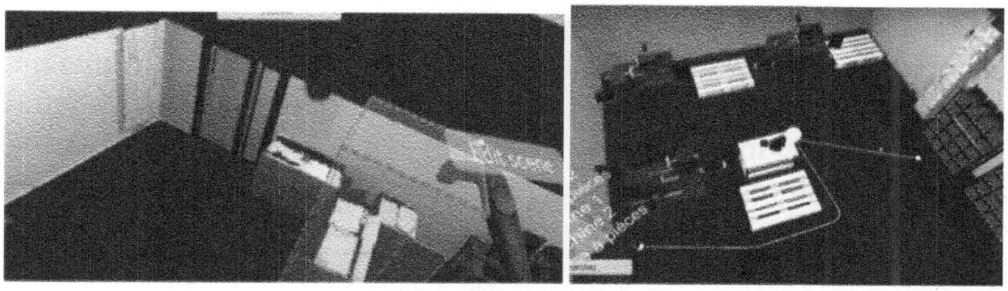

Figure 7.7. *Cokoon application developed by our team, allowing to cut freehand in a scanned point cloud in order to quickly test in virtual reality rearrangements of existing environments. For a color version of this figure, see www.iste.co.uk/fleury/innovation.zip*

Virtual reality applications can also be used as icebreakers or creative warm-up activities. Many virtual reality applications have an immediate fun aspect that lends itself well to this type of role. Participants can play an immersive "Pictionary" game and at the same time get to grips with the sketching tool that will be used for the next activity, but they can also find themselves in a fairy-tale environment (that you could not reproduce in real life) to gradually let go of the creative divergence activity to come.

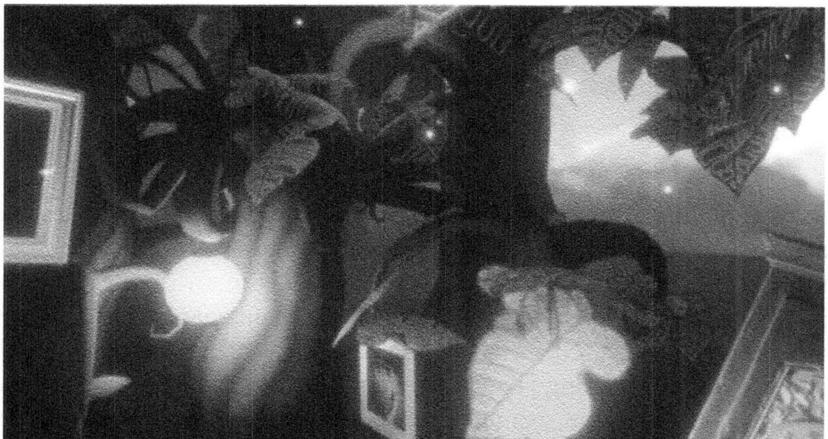

Figure 7.8. *Application "La plume et la lanterne" (the feather and the lantern) designed by students of Arts et Métiers as an immersive experience that is both playful and contemplative, conducive to letting go. For a color version of this figure, see www.iste.co.uk/fleury/innovation.zip*

Finally, virtual reality applications can play a role in terms of inspiration for ideation sessions. For example, one can imagine moving in a virtual showroom showing different vehicles before working on the improvement of a body, or in very different virtual apartments before working on a home automation device.

7.4. Choosing the right creativity tools

Based on the thesis work of Charles Mille (2020) conducted within our team, we have identified seven main factors determining the choice of the appropriate tool for a creative exercise: the type of project management, the individuals, the situation, the need for traceability, the geographical organization of the team, the level of progress of the project and the type of product/service designed.

Project management	Individuals	Situation	Traceability	Geographical organization	Project progress	Type of product/service
Lean Startup, UX Design, Time to Concept, etc	Profession, Motivation, Knowledge of methods, tools and domain, etc	On the move, unequipped, placed, etc	Need for archiving, technical constraint of storage and dissemination, etc	Total or partial regrouping, co-modality, asynchronous collaboration with persistent people, etc	Level of fidelity regarding productions, precision, etc	Need for visual representations, design standards, etc

Figure 7.9. *The seven categories of determinants of creativity tool choice*

The type of project management. This corresponds to constraints and to a general philosophy that indirectly implies certain choices of tools. Lean Startup was created to save a maximum of time and to allow for backtracking. This implies that the main characteristic of the tools that will be used in this type of project will be simplicity and speed. Design Thinking is a user-centered iterative approach in which we may be led, for example, to brainstorm directly with future end users. Thus, we may have to select tools for their affordances allowing novices to use them directly. The Time to Concept approach is specifically designed to integrate the uses of virtual reality. In particular, it leads to giving a lot of importance to the communicability of ideas because it necessarily implies a stage of communication of ideas between the experts and the client company.

Individuals. Depending on the individuals present, the type of tool that will support the ideation process will vary. A very innovative and stimulating tool can be a motivating vector to engage colleagues who are not very enthusiastic. Three types of individuals' knowledge are also to be taken into account:

– knowledge of creativity methods (participants used to creativity methods can more easily adapt to original approaches);

– the mastery of design or ideation tools (some tools are not very appropriate for novices, others are very accessible);

– and the knowledge of the field in which the future innovation takes place (if I have little knowledge, a collaborative tool allowing me to rely on more specialized colleagues can be beneficial).

Finally, the profession of the people involved is important because it is likely to determine to a large extent the points previously mentioned: motivation for the project and the three types of knowledge.

Situation. Many design professionals are accustomed to carrying a notebook with them at all times because they know that in their everyday lives, their brains continue to make associations outside the realm of consciousness and that an insight is likely to arise at any moment. The situation will thus contribute to determining the choice of tools. The designer in a restaurant with a client can be led to draw on the tablecloth if they find interesting ideas to explore together. It is then necessary to cut out the piece of tablecloth, or at least to take a picture of it! A designer who travels to a client's location does not necessarily have control over the room and the equipment they will have access to. In this case, they must deal with what they can carry and what they will find on site.

The need for traceability. As mentioned, during the design process, individuals are led to write down and sketch their ideas for different reasons. In general, this will serve as a medium for thinking about solving problems, as a medium for communicating ideas with colleagues, but also as a way of archiving the idea so that it can be taken up again in the next stages of the project. If you want to keep a record of the results of the workshop and depending on how you want to use this record afterward, the tool used will differ.

Geographical organization of the team. If the project team is grouped in a physical location, totally or partially, this leads to face-to-face, remote or co-modal creativity workshops. The type of tool used in the workshops is therefore strongly constrained from this point of view. Moreover, remote work can also imply a significant time difference, which naturally leads to asynchronous collaboration, making "persistent" tools essential, keeping track of the different participants.

The project's level of progress. The earlier the project is started, the less expensive the tools must be to make mistakes. Overall, the tools will have to become more accurate, and the prototypes more faithful, as the project progresses.

Type of product/service. The design of a new service lends itself less to visual representations than the design of a product. Moreover, certain domains of product design are extremely standardized, like the design of buildings or cars for example, which implies specific dedicated software that one does not necessarily find in other domains. In any case, these domains require more ideation in the form of sketches, whether they are made on paper, tablet or virtual reality, where service design can be both sketches and verbally expressed ideas. Environmental design will involve sketching while lending itself particularly well to virtual reality tools that allow direct immersion with a realistic perception of future spaces.

7.5. Immersive tools for innovation project stages

Immersive technologies can be used for different types of activities in an innovation project. Their potential and their role will also vary according to the type of project management in which the team is involved. Among the different virtual reality tools mentioned, some may appear in a very recurrent manner in projects, such as playful or inspirational applications. Other types of applications will be used in a more targeted way.

7.5.1. *Immersive technologies and Design Thinking*

The first steps of Design Thinking, empathy and definition, aim to identify a set of needs and to choose the one that we will try to satisfy. This generally involves user research methods such as questionnaire surveys, interviews or even activity analysis methods such as shadowing. For these different ways of approaching these stages, immersive technologies do not have any obvious added value. However, it is quite possible to deal with the empathy phase through divergent creativity exercises (participants have to list a maximum of needs/frustrations/difficulties related to their current user journey) and then the definition phase corresponds to convergence exercises (sorting of ideas, categorization, selection). For creative workshops of this type, virtual reality applications that allow brainstorming and sticking digital Post-it notes have their place, especially for remote workshops, or even asynchronous workshops in a same room (the Post-it notes of previous participants are hung on the wall when you enter the room). As for any creative activity, it is also possible to use a playful or contemplative application in an icebreaker or creative warm-up exercise to encourage letting go. The ideation stage aims to imagine a solution that will satisfy the need identified in the previous stage. Here again, ideation is classically carried out in the form of a divergence stage in which the collaborators imagine a large number of solutions, followed by a convergence stage in which they organize and select the solutions in order to choose those that will be prototyped. Immersive-storming applications have their place. We wish to add that when it comes to imagining solutions, in particular technical solutions, immersive sketching tools are particularly relevant. Moreover, contrary to the previous steps, participants may need additional knowledge or elements of inspiration.

The prototyping stage consists of creating a version of the technical solution or a representation that will allow it to be confronted with potential future users in order to enter a design-evaluation loop.

Generally speaking, this stage and the iterations with the testing phase lead to the design of low-fidelity prototypes at the beginning to reduce the time spent producing them in order to make mistakes at a lower cost and to increase the level of fidelity of the prototypes more or less progressively as the vision of the final product becomes clearer through testing. It is therefore a form of constant arbitration of the level of fidelity necessary according to the level of certainty and the time to be devoted to it. In some cases, certain virtual reality tools can lead to better compromises by increasing the fidelity of the prototype without necessarily increasing the workload to produce it. The contribution of virtual reality to these two stages depends on the nature of what is being produced (Wenzel and Meinel 2020). For example, it is understood that in the case of designing an additional feature of a mobile application, virtual reality will not be used for prototyping or testing. On the other hand, for many types of products or environments, virtual reality easily finds its place during these stages, as in the examples below.

The user *composes dashboards* (car, plane, boat, monitoring software) by manually dragging and resizing virtual components (speedometers of different types, lights, etc.). The testers are immersed and have to perform a task with this dashboard: either an interactive task if the application allows it (driving with the car on the virtual dashboard) or a cognitive task (finding such information quickly on the dashboard).

The user immerses himself or herself in the *scan of a building*, or even in the 3D model provided by the architects. They sketch freehand the layouts they plan to make and import 3D objects into the scene to position them. The testers will then immerse themselves to visit the place as it will have been fitted out to evaluate their feeling of space and the compatibility with what they will have to realize in this future place.

Future users immerse themselves in a virtual scene representing a *cruise ship cockpit* and they directly position what they imagine to be their workstation by taking into account and discussing constraints, such as so-and-so needs to see the sea from their workstation, so there should be no obstacle in front of them (Hollanti 2020).

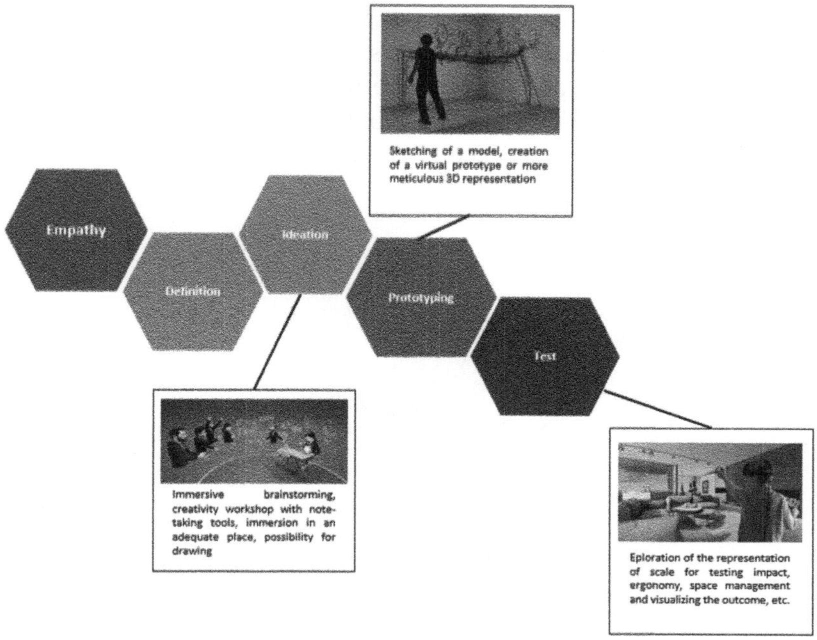

Figure 7.10. *Schematic representation of the uses of virtual reality in a Design Thinking project. For a color version of this figure, see www.iste.co.uk/fleury/innovation.zip*

7.5.2. *Immersive technologies and Lean Startup*

In the Lean Startup approach, the types of activities carried out with virtual reality tools are relatively similar to those mentioned above for Design Thinking, although the breakdown differs. In this approach, the applications for immersive-storming will intervene at the moment of hypothesis generation and selection. The immersive sketching tools will be used at the "build" stage to realize the Minimum Viable Product (MVP). During the "measure" stage, participants will be able to immerse themselves in the environment presenting the MVP in order to test it or visualize it to test their feelings. For example, the designer has sketched in virtual reality, or even modeled, a mobile wine cellar design based on the assumption that if the object is attractive enough, consumers will see an interest in having it in their living room (and therefore at the place of consumption). Potential future users immerse themselves in their scanned living room and position the mobile wine cellar where they want it and evaluate through a questionnaire the esthetic qualities, the practicality of the shape and their purchase intention.

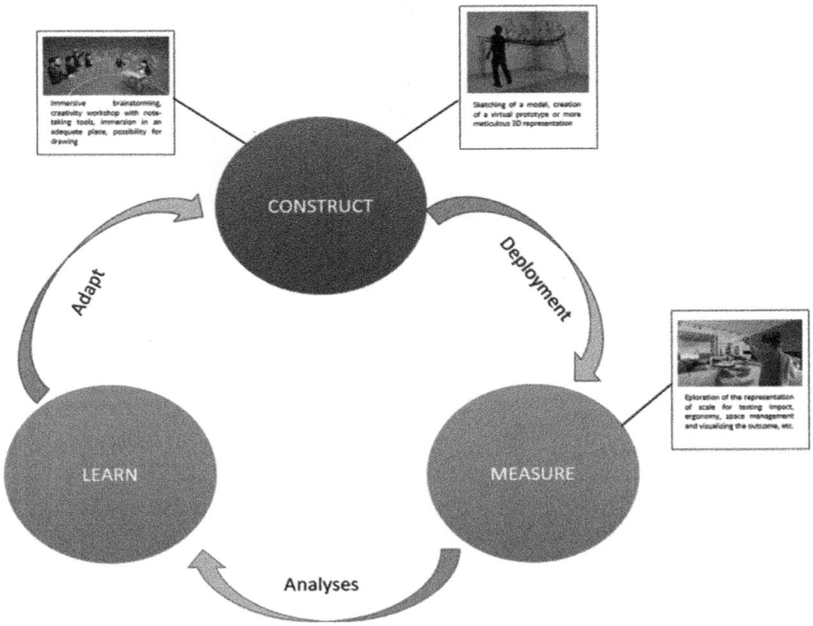

Figure 7.11. *Schematic representation of the uses of virtual reality in a Lean Startup project. For a color version of this figure, see www.iste.co.uk/fleury/innovation.zip*

7.5.3. *Immersive technologies and Time to Concept*

One of the particularities of the *Time to Concept* approach is that this method was designed within the framework of a chair on immersive technologies for innovation. This specificity explains why it is the method in which the integration of virtual reality technologies is most obvious. As explained above, the Time to Concept approach is particularly applicable as an open innovation approach in which experts will support a company in the identification of opportunities and the development of an innovative device. Brainstorming applications can be applied during the divergence and convergence stages. Convergence can also be supported by immersive sketching tools in co-creation between the experts and the company. Immersive 3D drawing tools can be used for prototyping and visualization/ interaction with a headset for the testing phase.

For example, let us imagine that a company manufacturing pleasure boats wants to explore the opportunities linked to connected objects for possible future innovations. It does not have the internal skills and does not know if this is a promising avenue, so it cannot consider a specific recruitment at this stage. It then decided to deploy an open innovation process with the Time to Concept approach. Specialists in innovation methods help them to implement the approach. They contact experts in connected objects with real technical knowledge. These experts start by getting together to carry out immersive-storming on innovation ideas for the company, using virtual environments as inspiration media. Their ideas will come more easily if they brainstorm on a virtual marina, on a boat at sea, or in a production plant. After that, they will visit the company and exchange on their problems, then they will adjust their concepts on the points that were not relevant. The experts and the company then meet again for an immersive-storming in the most appropriate environment. If the ideas correspond to on-board applications, they can use a 3D model of a boat to present, select and refine them. To do this, they can use the sketching and 3D modeling functions. Thus, experts can represent bold ideas and people from the company can directly correct them, adjust them, so that it better takes into account the constraints. When the partners share the same vision, more precise virtual reality modeling tools can be mobilized, or even the addition of simple interactions or sound elements, for example, to make it testable.

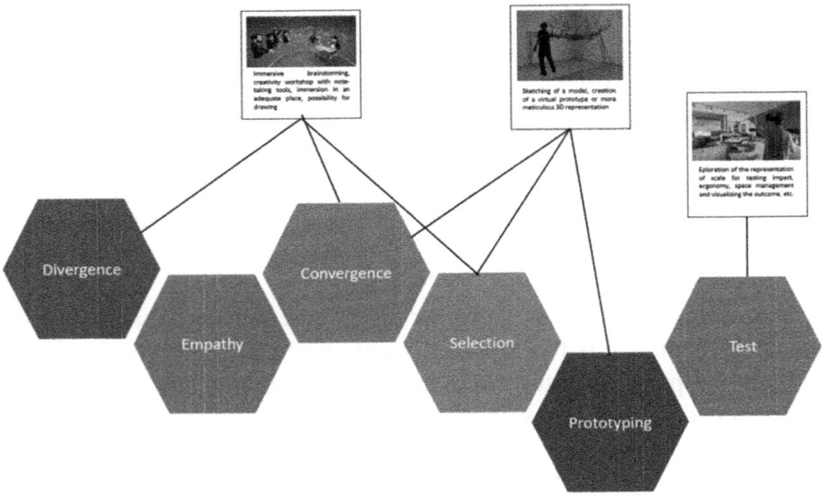

Figure 7.12. *Schematic representation of the uses of virtual reality in a project conducted with the Time to Concept approach. For a color version of this figure, see www.iste.co.uk/fleury/innovation.zip*

7.5.4. *Immersive technologies and the creative process*

We examined the moments of intervention of immersive technologies in the conduct of projects according to the stages of the project. If we no longer look at things on the scale of the project, but rather on the scale of the creative process and therefore of the stages that are generally reproduced more or less directly during creativity workshops, we see that virtual reality will intervene both in regard to individual and group activities. According to Graessler and Taplick (2019), the stages of preparation, individual and group idea generation and idea validation can benefit considerably from the contribution of immersive technologies.

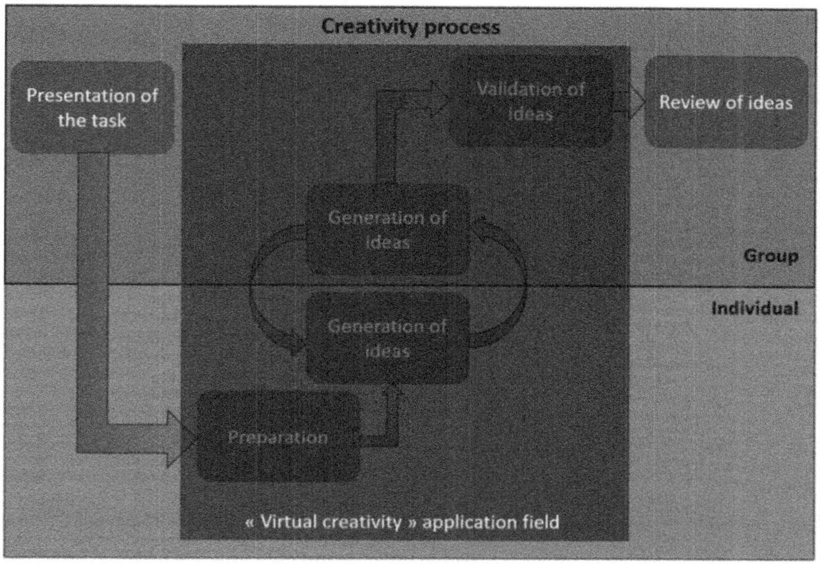

Figure 7.13. *Representation of the stages in which virtual reality applications intervene in a creativity workshop (according to Graessler and Taplick 2019). For a color version of this figure, see www.iste.co.uk/fleury/innovation.zip*

8

A Successful Immersive Experience for More Creativity

A permanent confrontation between theory and experience is a necessary condition for the expression of creativity.
PIERRE JOLIOT

8.1. The experience of immersed users

Coming to grips with immersive technologies is not always easy. It is relatively natural to guide a user who is using a mobile application, a Website or a computer software because on screens we are able to see what the user sees and does and we can therefore guide him or her by pointing to elements on the screen. In virtual reality, the user cannot see you if you are next to him or her. It is therefore impossible to show him or her something, to really guide him or her. The quality of the ergonomics of virtual reality applications is therefore even more crucial. Ergonomics and good practices to generate a quality user experience have been widely developed in the web domain, first on computers with keyboard/mouse usage. The singular characteristics of mobile devices, smartphones and tablets have given rise to new recommendations specific to these smaller touch screens, and intended for use by users who potentially do other things with their main hand and with part of their cognitive resources. This new category of hardware has radically changed the ergonomic constraints of virtual interface design.

8.1.1. *Drawing inspiration from reality*

An even more radical change in the approach to usability is emerging with the development of immersive technologies. Of course, we are not starting from scratch, but if user experience specialists are able to answer almost any ergonomic question for a PC or mobile interface, the unknown part in the field of virtual reality is still very important, thus constituting a vast territory to explore, not yet completely standardized.

The user of a virtual reality application is potentially standing and walking and that can in itself constitute, not a competing activity, but a form of interaction with the application. The viewing and interaction area is 360°. The question of organizing information in a limited screen no longer makes sense. In web ergonomics, it was already commonplace to draw inspiration from the tangible world to design virtual interfaces that are easy to understand by users because they refer to already acquired reference points. This is the case, for example, with Material Design. Because the correspondence between gesture and result is even stronger in virtual reality, being inspired by the real world to design applications is even more relevant to make interactions natural. An essential difference between virtual reality applications and mobile applications is that the former is supposed to lead the user to adhere, to "believe" that he or she is in a reality other than the tangible reality in which he or she evolves daily. He or she must have the feeling of being present in the virtual environment of the application. We can make the parallel with the phenomenon of suspension of disbelief coming from the world of novels and movies. The user knows that what he or she sees is not the tangible reality, but if he or she adheres to it, he or she accepts suspending this disbelief, thus to make as if he or she did not know that this reality was virtual and he or she will thus interact with the objects and feel emotions according to what he or she will experience in this environment.

8.1.2. *A future standardization*

While virtual reality is, for the moment, less standardized than the web, there are nevertheless ergonomic criteria applicable to these applications. First of all, as for any technology with which humans interact, the criteria of Bastien and Scapin (1995), although not specific, apply perfectly. Some of their criteria are even more important. For example, the homogeneity and coherence of using the same codes and interaction modalities throughout the experience are even more essential in virtual reality. In the same way, the general criterion of guidance is particularly essential in virtual reality. Guidance is comparable to a form of politeness. When you receive a guest in your home, you have to tell them what they can do, where they can sit, where they can put down their jacket, where they can get a drink, etc. In virtual reality, it is the same thing: the user who arrives in the application does not know what he or she can or cannot do. It is therefore a matter of skillfully using affordances or explicit indications to guide them and show them what actions can be performed. The general ergonomic criteria of Bastien and Scapin (1995) have been enriched by criteria specific to virtual reality by Bach and Scapin (2003).

8.1.3. *User support*

In any case, when you bring an individual to use a virtual reality tool for the first time, he or she will have to be supported. This support must reduce as much as possible the time he or she will spend being disoriented and trying to find what to do or how to do it. The demand for usability and learning time is constantly increasing. Today, if a user has to spend a few minutes fumbling with an application, he or she will tend to think that it is not practical to use. It is therefore important to ensure that users can immediately grasp the interaction methods, the application's universe and the graphic charter. In some cases, you use an application with a self-sufficient tutorial to allow for easy appropriation. This is the only case in which your introductory presentation of the tool can be relatively brief.

Concerning the interaction modalities, there is a tendency to think that the person should be guided by voice while manipulating the tool with the headset on. This is a mistake. A novice participant is not familiar with the controller, has not identified the buttons or joysticks and will not be able to obey instructions because of this. The most effective solution is to give the participant a joystick and take one yourself in order to demonstrate the different gestures and buttons by asking him or her to imitate you, while naming the different interaction modalities in a simple way so that you can reuse these terms later ("press the trigger with the index finger", "use the joystick via the push button", etc.). Once you understand the commands, you can explain the main interactions: how to move in the scene, open the menu, grab an object, etc. As for most of the activities you will lead in creative workshops, it is also important to explain in a transparent way, before the participants are using headphones, what the nature and the goal of the experience they are going to receive and what is expected from them in this context. It is important to keep in mind that for novices there may be a certain fear of not understanding what they will have to do and of making fools of themselves in front of their colleagues. It is important to take this risk into account, both by adopting a benevolent and reassuring posture and by taking the time needed for everyone to fully grasp the tool. It is also important to make sure that everyone is busy to avoid having "spectators" who will observe the users of the immersive application by making comments. Finally, just like software on screen or a Website, an immersive application has a form of graphic charter, language and color codes. These different elements must be introduced to the participants beforehand if the tutorial does not do so explicitly. This can be done by showing screenshots of the application in a slide show so that everyone can visualize the codes before putting on the headset. Any difficulty of the participants once they have the headset could be badly experienced and will be more difficult for you to manage. Also, when participants are using the tool for the first time, do not hesitate to focus the presentation on the most important features, leaving out some of the more secondary features that can be explored later.

To a certain extent, the level of precautions to be taken when introducing the immersive tools can be more moderate in the case where the people concerned are not novices in the use of virtual reality. A good practice is, after the tutorial, to directly start a playful exercise in the virtual reality tool in order to take it in hand without being in the real exercise yet. This pre-exercise, if it is well chosen, plays the role of both a creative warm-up and training in the use of the tool. The ideal is to choose an exercise that will lead to the use of the tool's functions, that is fun and creative. Typically, if your tool allows you to stick virtual Post-it notes of different colors on the walls, you can for example ask each sub-group to cover a wall in order to make a mosaic using the company's colors.

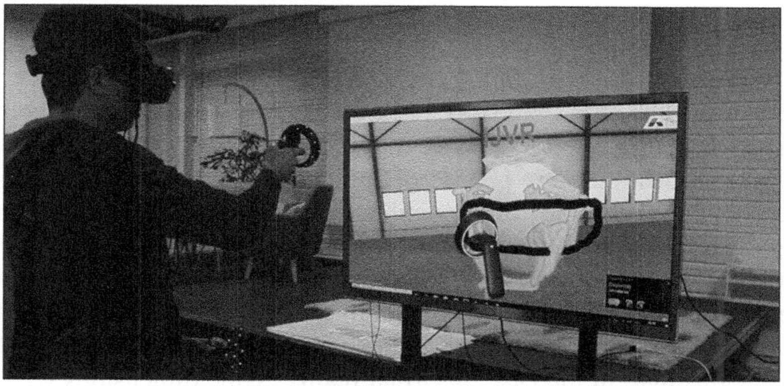

Figure 8.1. *Example of an exercise used in our team to learn about Time2Sketch, our immersive drawing tool. The participants have to imagine and draw a logo for their team. For a color version of this figure, see www.iste.co.uk/fleury/innovation.zip*

8.1.4. *Physical space planning*

The layout of the place, the physical space, must be compatible with the virtual reality application used. Some applications require little physical movement while others require a lot. In some cases, teleportation devices can solve the problem. Some users tend to be anxious about the risk of bumping into each other and this is very detrimental to their immersion. Therefore, before they are using the headset, it is best to show them the real space and how they can find their way around in the virtual space to avoid bumping into each other. Often, novice users tend to remain relatively static not only in their movements, but also in their head movements. Sometimes it will be necessary to invite users to move and turn their heads, or to design the application so that it induces these behaviors in a subtle way. For example, if a virtual object moves around the user, he or she will tend to follow it with his or her eyes and thus notice that he or she can look around. Another possibility is to have large objects directly in the visual field that induce head movements to look at them in full. For example, if I see a vertical tree trunk in front of me, I will likely look up to look at the rest of the tree.

8.1.5. *The psychological dimensions of the user experience*

According to the ISO 9241-210 standard, user experience is defined as "the user's physical, cognitive and emotional responses that result from the use of a system, product or service". Hassenzahl (2001) proposes a more precise definition by breaking down the user experience according to several criteria: hedonic qualities and ergonomic qualities that simultaneously lead the user to generate a judgment of attractiveness, this judgment then determining his or her behaviors and emotions. This model of user experience is not specific to immersive technologies. It is rather considered for web interfaces. It is obvious that, in the case of virtual reality, same dimensions will be important to determine the user experience, but it is also obvious that some other aspects will also come into play, such as the physical characteristics of the headsets or the feeling of presence. At the time of writing, several authors are carrying out structural statistical modeling of the factors influencing user experience in virtual reality, but none of this work has yet resulted in a stabilized and operational model. However, these works already give us an idea of the variables taken into account to explain the user experience in virtual reality.

In 2007, Lin and Parker evaluated the user experience of participants using an immersive entertainment application. The variables emphasized were presence, enjoyment, simulator evil, engagement, immersion and active interactivity mode. A similar study conducted by Shina *et al.* (2013) focused on a virtual learning environment. It was based on the following components: immersion, sense of presence, flow, satisfaction, perceived usefulness, perceived usability and previous user experiences. Cheng *et al.* (2014) emphasized the importance of flow, influenced by interactivity, user skills or attention. Finally, Tcha-Tokey *et al.* (2018) have advanced toward an integrative model in which we find globally the same variables including flow, perceived usability, skills, emotions, presence, immersion or engagement.

8.2. The creative's user experience

The work on user experience in virtual reality mentioned above is built on measurements taken in a game or learning situation, but not in a creative activity. This also raises the question of the links between creative performance and user experience. The user experience depends largely on the work situation, the hardware used, and these elements then determine the effectiveness or efficiency of the creative activity.

Figure 8.2. *Example of a collaborative work situation at the Institut Arts et Métiers de Laval, with a user creating three-dimensional animations in virtual reality, assisted by his or her colleague visualizing the result in the room in augmented reality. For a color version of this figure, see www.iste.co.uk/fleury/innovation.zip*

8.2.1. *The Creative Support Index*

In MacDonald *et al.*'s (2006) study, participants were asked to get together to compose music. At each work session, they had to fill in a questionnaire measuring their level of flow (Csikszentmihalyi and Csikszentmihalyi 1988). At the end, the creative character of the created music was evaluated. The study shows a strong correlation between flow and creativity. Flow thus appears as a possible determinant of creative performance. Flow is often linked to user experience in the literature. Zhou (2013) went so far as to choose to measure user experience in his study by measuring only flow, while Bernhaupt *et al.* (2007) describe the user experience of video games as the result of several factors, including playability, usability and flow.

Cherry and Latulipe (2014) designed the Creativity Support Index, a questionnaire aimed at assessing the perception of tools for creativity. The dimensions selected in this questionnaire were:

– *results worth effort* (satisfaction with the result in relation to the effort, perceived efficiency);

– *exploration* (the system allows you to explore different ideas);

– *collaboration* (easy to share ideas);

– *immersion* (leads to being absorbed in the activity);

– *expressiveness* (allows you to feel creative during use);

– *enjoyment* (pleasure of use).

Lecossier *et al.* (2019) explicitly introduced user experience into the field of innovation research. It is about looking at the experience of people who mobilize innovation methodologies.

8.2.2. *The design of tools for ideation*

Graessler and Taplick (2019) proposed a guideline regarding the design of virtual reality tools for ideation. This guideline consists of a set of recommendations described below.

Hardware architecture: to generate and represent ideas, participants must be able to interact with the virtual environment. They must be able to move (walk, teleport) and grasp objects. Interactions between project members must be possible through different channels, voice, gestures or text messaging. The visualization will ideally simulate human senses. The virtual reality headset is a good solution for visual stimuli. The olfactory and haptic stimuli are very interesting, but require specific materials that are not currently standardized and widespread. Finally, the authors underline the importance of the integration of the tool in the network in the sense that the tool must work without error or interruption in the team.

The functionalities of the tool: a virtual environment configurator based on a content database is an appropriate tool to help not only in the preparation phase of the workshop, but also in the generation of ideas. This environment configurator must allow for not only importing objects, but also setting their parameters (sizes, colors, textures, etc.). It must also be possible to choose the "Skybox" (texture that encompasses the virtual environment). Modeling tools are also required to generate objects or concepts that are not in the content base and to enhance existing objects. Sketching tools are particularly interesting because they allow live visualization of the generated ideas. A virtual whiteboard can also be used to improve ideas in a group setting as would a tangible whiteboard, but with possible remote use. As Mille (2020) points out, the ideas generated must be able to be archived and documented. The tool must therefore make it possible to generate different media that can be reused or re-consulted, thus generating screenshots, videos with sound commentary. Finally, the tools must facilitate communication between the workshop participants. They must therefore allow users to embody their avatars and to communicate orally in a natural way.

The content of the configurators and modeling tools (virtual objects, textures, materials, shapes) must be appropriate to the themes being addressed. For example, if we are working on the layout of a monitoring room, we can imagine the possibility of modeling screens of any size with a simple gesture.

The *usability* of the tools must be high to promote easy use.

Stimulation through virtual reality aims at making participants generate more ideas. It mainly involves a wide spectrum of visual stimuli based on the presence and combination of virtual objects, textures, materials and images. The addition of tactile, auditory and olfactory elements can also improve the impression of realism and lead to associations that can lead to relevant ideas.

User-specific features refer primarily to the level of tool complexity. If users are using the tool for the first time, for example, it may be best to present and use only the main features to simplify ownership.

Spatial infrastructure: the level of spatial constraints in the virtual environment should be as low as possible. Empty spaces can be used to store the participants' achievements, while the "designed" spaces can be used as areas to stimulate the participants' creativity.

Enjoyability and playfulness are important elements in creating an atmosphere conducive to letting go, increasing acceptance of the activity and intrinsic motivation, which we know (Amabile 1983) is a strong factor in creativity.

Conclusion

In the introduction to this book, we wrote about the importance of innovation and the ongoing digital transformation. The objective of this book is to bring a scientific insight on how to integrate immersive technologies in the practice of the first steps of innovation, in the workshops of creativity in all their forms. It aims to provide innovation managers, project managers, company directors, etc., with a global vision and a set of tools that make the most of the enormous potential of immersive technologies (Virtual, Mixed or Augmented Reality, gathered under the acronym "XR") in the field of designing new products/services/industrial processes/environments.

Creativity is a complex phenomenon. To make a team creative, it is necessary to master the different techniques of both workshop facilitation and team management as well as project management, in order to select the most relevant approach for each problem. It is also essential to be able to select the most appropriate technologies and to integrate them in an innovative and coherent way. This approach must promote the acceptability of these technologies within the teams, collective intelligence and the ability to generate disruptive innovations. Neglecting immersive technologies for ideation means missing out on the opportunity to improve your creativity practices to accelerate the innovation process in your company. On the contrary, engaging your company on the path of innovation equipped with digital technologies will lead you to be part of the global community of innovation 4.0 precursors.

References

Agnès, A., Fleury, S., Auzerais, A., Bisson, I., Dulau, E., Buisine, S., Richir, S. (2020). Text input tools' complementarity in immersive virtual environments. *International Journal of Design and Innovation Research.*

Alawad, A. (2012). Can we bring the natural environment into the art classroom? Can natural sound foster creativity? *Educational Research and Reviews*, 7(28), 627–631.

Alencar, E.M. and Bruno-Faria, M.F. (1997). Characteristics of an organizational environment which stimulate and inhibit creativity. *The Journal of Creative Behavior*, 31(4), 271–281.

Amabile, T.M. (1983). The social psychology of creativity: A componential conceptualization. *Journal of Personality and Social Psychology*, 45(2), 357.

Amabile, T.M. (1988). A model of creativity and innovation in organizations. *Research in Organizational Behavior*, 10(1), 123–167.

Andolfi, V.R., Di Nuzzo, C., Antonietti, A. (2017). Opening the mind through the body: The effects of posture on creative processes. *Thinking Skills and Creativity*, 24, 20–28.

Antons, D. and Piller, F.T. (2015). Opening the black box of "Not Invented Here": Attitudes, decision biases, and behavioral consequences. *Academy of Management Perspectives*, 29(2), 193–217.

Arnaldi, B., Guitton, P., Moreau, G. (eds) (2018). *Virtual Reality and Augmented Reality: Myths and Realities*. ISTE Ltd, London, and John Wiley & Sons, Hoboken, NJ, USA.

Atchley, R.A., Strayer, D.L., Atchley, P. (2012). Creativity in the wild: Improving creative reasoning through immersion in natural settings. *PloS One*, 7(12), e51474.

Baas, M., De Dreu, C.K., Nijstad, B.A. (2008). A meta-analysis of 25 years of mood-creativity research: Hedonic tone, activation, or regulatory focus? *Psychological Bulletin*, 134(6), 779.

Bach, C. and Scapin, D. (2003). Ergonomic criteria adapted to human virtual environment interaction. In *Proceedings of the 15th Conference on l'Interaction Homme-Machine*, 24–31. Association for Computing Machinery, New York, USA.

Baird, B., Smallwood, J., Mrazek, M.D., Kam, J.W., Franklin, M.S., Schooler, J.W. (2012). Inspired by distraction: Mind wandering facilitates creative incubation. *Psychological Science*, 23(10), 1117–1122.

Bastien, J.C. and Scapin, D.L. (1995). Evaluating a user interface with ergonomic criteria. *International Journal of Human-Computer Interaction*, 7(2), 105–121.

Bateson, P., Bateson, P.P.G., Martin, P. (2013). *Play, Playfulness, Creativity and Innovation*. Cambridge University Press, Cambridge, United Kingdom.

Batey, M., Chamorro-Premuzic, T., Furnham, A. (2010). Individual differences in ideational behavior: Can the Big Five and psychometric intelligence predict creativity scores? *Creativity Research Journal*, 22(1), 90–97.

Baumann, O., Borra, R.J., Bower, J.M., Cullen, K.E., Habas, C., Ivry, R.B., Leggio, M., Mattingley, J.B., Molinari, M., Moulton, E.A., Paulin, M.G., Pavlova, M.A., Schmahmann, J.D., Sokolov, A.A. (2015). Consensus paper: The role of the cerebellum in perceptual processes. *The Cerebellum*, 14(2), 197–220.

Bereitschaft, B. (2018). Mapping creative spaces in Omaha, NE: Resident perceptions versus creative firm locations. *ISPRS International Journal of Geo-Information*, 7(7), 263.

Berman, M.G., Jonides, J., Kaplan, S. (2008). The cognitive benefits of interacting with nature. *Psychological Science*, 19(12), 1207–1212.

Bernhaupt, R., Eckschlager, M., Tscheligi, M. (2007). Methods for evaluating games: How to measure usability and user experience in games? In *Proceedings of the International Conference on Advances in Computer Entertainment Technology*, 309–310. ACM, New York, USA.

Berto, R. (2005). Exposure to restorative environments helps restore attentional capacity. *Journal of Environmental Psychology*, 25(3), 249–259.

Berto, R., Baroni, M.R., Zainaghi, A., Bettella, S. (2010). An exploratory study of the effect of high and low fascination environments on attentional fatigue. *Journal of Environmental Psychology*, 30(4), 494–500.

Bertoline, G.R. (1999). *Technical Graphics and Communications.* Mcgraw-Hill College, New York, USA.

Bessière, K., Seay, A.F., Kiesler, S. (2007). The ideal elf: Identity exploration in World of Warcraft. *Cyberpsychology & Behavior*, 10(4), 530–535.

Beukeboom, C.J., Langeveld, D., Tanja-Dijkstra, K. (2012). Stress-reducing effects of real and artificial nature in a hospital waiting room. *The Journal of Alternative and Complementary Medicine*, 18(4), 329–333.

Bouchard, C., Aoussat, A., Duchamp, R. (2006). Role of sketching in conceptual design of car styling. *Journal of Design Research*, 5(1), 116–148.

Bowman, D.A. and McMahan, R.P. (2007). Virtual reality: How much immersion is enough? *Computer*, 40(7), 36–43.

Bringslimark, T., Hartig, T., Patil, G.G. (2007). Psychological benefits of indoor plants in workplaces: Putting experimental results into context. *HortScience*, 42(3), 581–587.

Brissenden, J.A. and Somers, D.C. (2019). Cortico–cerebellar networks for visual attention and working memory. *Current Opinion in Psychology*, 29, 239–247.

Buchanan, L.B. (1998). The impact of Big Five personality characteristics on group cohesion and creative task performance. Doctoral Dissertation, Virginia Tech, Blacksburg, VA, USA.

Buisine, S., Guegan, J., Barré, J., Segonds, F., Aoussat, A. (2016). Using avatars to tailor ideation process to innovation strategy. *Cognition, Technology & Work*, 18(3), 583–594.

Buxton, B. (2010). *Sketching User Experiences: Getting the Design Right and the Right Design.* Morgan Kaufmann. San Francisco, CA, USA.

Calderon-Hernandez, C., Paes, D., Irizarry, J., Brioso, X. (2019). Comparing virtual reality and 2-dimensional drawings for the visualization of a construction project. In *Computing in Civil Engineering 2019: Visualization, Information Modeling, and Simulation*. American Society of Civil Engineers, Reston, VA, USA, 17–24.

Carlson, K.A. (2011). The impact of humor on memory: Is the humor effect about humor? *Humor*, 24(1), 21–41.

Casakin, H. (2004). Visual analogy as a cognitive strategy in the design process. Expert versus novice performance. *Journal of Design Research*, 4(2), 197–217.

Ceylan, C., Dul, J., Aytac, S. (2008). Can the office environment stimulate a manager's creativity? *Human Factors and Ergonomics in Manufacturing & Service Industries*, 18(6), 589–602.

Chamorro-Premuzic, T. and Reichenbacher, L. (2008). Effects of personality and threat of evaluation on divergent and convergent thinking. *Journal of Research in Personality*, 42(4), 1095–1101.

Cheng, L.K., Chieng, M.H., Chieng, W.H. (2014). Measuring virtual experience in a three-dimensional virtual reality interactive simulator environment: A structural equation modeling approach. *Virtual Reality*, 18(3), 173–188.

Cherry, E. and Latulipe, C. (2014). Quantifying the creativity support of digital tools through the creativity support index. *ACM Transactions on Computer-Human Interaction (TOCHI)*, 21(4), 21.

Chesbrough, H.W. (2003). *Open Innovation: The New Imperative for Creating and Profiting from Technology*. Harvard Business Press, Boston, MA, USA.

Choo, P.K., Lou, Z.N., Camburn, B.A., Wood, K.L., Koo, B., Grey, F. (2014). Ideation methods: A first study on measured outcomes with personality type. *ASME 2014 International Design Engineering Technical Conferences and Computers and Information in Engineering Conference*, American Society of Mechanical Engineers Digital Collection. New York, USA.

Cross, N. (1999). Natural intelligence in design. *Design Studies*, 20(1), 25–39.

Cross, N. and Roy, R. (1989). *Engineering Design Methods*, Volume 4. Wiley, New York, USA.

Csikszentmihalyi, M. (1999). Implications of a systems perspective for the study of creativity. In *Handbook of Creativity*, Sternberg, R.J. (ed.), Cambridge University Press, Cambridge, United Kingdom.

Csikszentmihalyi, M. and Csikszentmihalyi, I.S. (1988). *Optimal Experience: Psychological Studies of Flow in Consciousness*. Cambridge University Press, Cambridge, United Kingdom.

De Dreu, C.K., Baas, M., Nijstad, B.A. (2008). Hedonic tone and activation level in the mood-creativity link: Toward a dual pathway to creativity model. *Journal of Personality and Social Psychology*, 94(5), 739.

Diana, L., Frei, M., Chesham, A., de Jong, D., Chiffi, K., Nyffeler, T., Bassetti, C.L., Goebel, N., Eberhard-Moscicka, A.K., Müri, R.M. (2021). A divergent approach to pareidolias – Exploring creativity in a novel way. *Psychology of Aesthetics, Creativity, and the Arts*, 15(2), 313–323 [Online]. Available at: https://doi.org/10.1037/aca0000293.

Do, A.M., Rupert, A.V., Wolford, G. (2008). Evaluations of pleasurable experiences: The peak-end rule. *Psychonomic Bulletin & Review*, 15(1), 96–98.

Dorta, T.V. (2004). Drafted virtual reality: A new paradigm to design with computers. *Proceedings of the 9th International Conference on Computer Aided Architectural Design Research in Asia*. 28–30 April, Seoul Korea, 829–844.

Dorta, T.V., Safin, S., Boudhraâ, S., Marchand, E.B. (2019). CO-DESIGNING IN SOCIAL VR. Process awareness and suitable representations to empower user participation. arXiv preprint: arXiv:1906.11004.

Drey, T., Gugenheimer, J., Karlbauer, J., Milo, M., Rukzio, E. (2020). VRSketchIn: Exploring the design space of pen and tablet interaction for 3D sketching in virtual reality. *Proceedings of the 2020 CHI Conference on Human Factors in Computing Systems*, Association for Computing Machinery, New York, USA, 1–14.

Dul, J. and Ceylan, C. (2011). Work environments for employee creativity. *Ergonomics*, 54(1), 12–20.

Dul, J. and Ceylan, C. (2014). The impact of a creativity-supporting work environment on a firm's product innovation performance. *Journal of Product Innovation Management*, 31(6), 1254–1267.

Dul, J., Ceylan, C., Jaspers, F. (2011). Knowledge workers' creativity and the role of the physical work environment. *Human Resource Management*, 50(6), 715–734.

Dunn, R.A. and Guadagno, R.E. (2012). My avatar and me – Gender and personality predictors of avatar-self discrepancy. *Computers in Human Behavior*, 28(1), 97–106.

Dunning, D., Johnson, K., Ehrlinger, J., Kruger, J. (2003). Why people fail to recognize their own incompetence. *Current Directions in Psychological Science*, 12, 83–87.

Durling, D., Cross, N., Johnson, J. (1996). Personality and learning preferences of students in design and design-related disciplines. In *IDATER 96 Conference*, Smith, J.S. (ed.). Loughborough University, Loughborough, United Kingdom.

Ekströmer, P., Wever, R., Andersson, P., Jönsson, J. (2019). Shedding light on game engines and virtual reality for design ideation. *Proceedings of the 22nd International Conference on Engineering Design (ICED19)*, The Cambridge Academic Press, Cambridge, United Kingdom.

Escera, C., Yago, E., Corral, M.J., Corbera, S., Nuñez, M.I. (2003). Attention capture by auditory significant stimuli: Semantic analysis follows attention switching. *European Journal of Neuroscience*, 18(8), 2408–2412.

Feeman, S.M., Wright, L.B., Salmon, J.L. (2018). Exploration and evaluation of CAD modeling in virtual reality. *Computer-Aided Design and Applications*, 15(6), 892–904.

Ferraro III, F.M. (2015). Enhancement of convergent creativity following a multiday wilderness experience. *Ecopsychology*, 7(1), 7–11.

Finch, L., Tomiyama, A., Ward, A. (2017). Taking a stand: The effects of standing desks on task performance and engagement. *International Journal of Environmental Research and Public Health*, 14(8), 939.

Finke, R.A., Ward, T.B., Smith, S.M. (1992). *Creative Cognition: Theory, Research, and Applications*. The MIT Press. Cambridge, MA, USA.

Fleury, S., Agnès, A., Cados, L., Denis-Lutard, Q., Duchêne, C., Rigaud, N., Richir, S. (2020a). Effects of social influence on idea selection in creativity workshops. *Thinking Skills and Creativity*, 100691.

Fleury, S., Agnès, A., Vanukuru, R., Goumillout, E., Delcombel, N., Richir, S. (2020b). Studying the effects of visual movement on creativity. *Thinking Skills and Creativity*, 100661.

Frith, E. and Loprinzi, P.D. (2018). Experimental effects of acute exercise and music listening on cognitive creativity. *Physiology & Behavior*, 191, 21–28.

Fromm, J., Mirbabaie, M., Stieglitz, S. (2020). The effects of virtual reality affordances and constraints on negative group effects during brainstorming sessions. *15th International Conference on Wirtschaftsinformatik*, Potsdam, Germany, March.

Funder, D.C. (2001). *The Personality Puzzle*. Norton, New York.

Furnham, A. and Yazdanpanahi, T. (1995). Personality differences and group versus individual brainstorming. *Personality and Individual Differences*, 19(1), 73–80.

Gilson, N.D., Hall, C., Renton, A., Ng, N., Von Hippel, W. (2017). Do sitting, standing, or treadmill desks impact psychobiological indicators of work productivity? *Journal of Physical Activity and Health*, 14(10), 793–796.

Goel, V. (1995). *Sketches of Thought*. MIT Press. Cambridge, MA, USA.

Goldschmidt, G. (1992). Serial sketching: Visual problem solving in designing. *Cybernetics and System*, 23(2), 191–219.

Goldschmidt, G. and Smolkov, M. (2006). Variances in the impact of visual stimuli on design problem solving performance. *Design Studies*, 27(5), 549–569.

Gonen-Yaacovi, G., De Souza, L.C., Levy, R., Urbanski, M., Josse, G., Volle, E. (2013). Rostral and caudal prefrontal contribution to creativity: A meta-analysis of functional imaging data. *Frontiers in Human Neuroscience*, 7, 465 [Online]. Available at: https://doi.org/10.3389/fnhum.2013.00465.

Gorisse, G., Dubosc, C., Christmann, O., Fleury., S., Poinsot, K., Richir, S. (2020). Effect of avatar anthropomorphism on body ownership, attractiveness and collaboration in immersive virtual environments. *International Conference on Artificial Reality and Telexistence & Eurographics Symposium on Virtual Environments*. The Eurographics Association, Norrköping, Sweden.

Graessler, I. and Taplick, P. (2019). Supporting creativity with virtual reality technology. *Proceedings of the 22nd International Conference on Engineering Design (ICED19)*. Cambridge University Press, Cambridge, United Kingdom.

Guegan, J., Buisine, S., Mantelet, F., Maranzana, N., Segonds, F. (2016). Avatar-mediated creativity: When embodying inventors makes engineers more creative. *Computers in Human Behavior*, 61, 165–175.

Guegan, J., Segonds, F., Barré, J., Maranzana, N., Mantelet, F., Buisine, S. (2017). Social identity cues to improve creativity and identification in face-to-face and virtual groups. *Computers in Human Behavior*, 77, 140–147.

Halfhill, T., Sundstrom, E., Lahner, J., Calderone, W., Nielsen, T.M. (2005). Group personality composition and group effectiveness: An integrative review of empirical research. *Small Group Research*, 36(1), 83–105.

Hallihan, G.M., Cheong, H., Shu, L.H. (2012). Confirmation and cognitive bias in design cognition. *International Design Engineering Technical Conferences and Computers and Information in Engineering Conference*, ASME, New York, USA, 45066, 913–924.

Haner, U.E. (2005). Spaces for creativity and innovation in two established organizations. *Creativity and Innovation Management*, 14(3), 288–298.

Hao, N., Xue, H., Yuan, H., Wang, Q., Runco, M.A. (2017). Enhancing creativity: Proper body posture meets proper emotion. *Acta Psychologica*, 173, 32–40.

Hartig, T., Mang, M., Evans, G.W. (1991). Restorative effects of natural environment experiences. *Environment and Behavior*, 23(1), 3–26.

Hartig, T., Evans, G.W., Jamner, L.D., Davis, D.S., Gärling, T. (2003). Tracking restoration in natural and urban field settings. *Journal of Environmental Psychology*, 23(2), 109–123.

Hassenzahl, M. (2001). The effect of perceived hedonic quality on product appealingness. *International Journal of Human-Computer Interaction*, 13(4), 481–499.

Hatchuel, A. and Weil, B. (2002). CK theory. *Proceedings of the Herbert Simon International Conference on Design Sciences*, 15(3), 1–16.

Hatchuel, A. and Weil, B. (2009). CK design theory: An advanced formulation. *Research in Engineering Design*, 19(4), 181.

Hatchuel, A., Le Masson, P., Weil, B. (2000). Co-development to the test of intensive innovation: Towards new forms of organisation for innovative design in the case of car manufacturers and component makers. *8th GERPISA International Colloquium The World that Changed: the Machine: The Future of the Auto Industry for the 21st Century*, Paris.

Heerwagen, J.H. and Orians, G.H. (1986). Adaptations to windowlessness: A study of the use of visual decor in windowed and windowless offices. *Environment and Behavior*, 18(5), 623–639.

Hoff, E.V. and Öberg, N.K. (2015). The role of the physical work environment for creative employees: A case study of digital artists. *The International Journal of Human Resource Management*, 26(14), 1889–1906.

Hollanti, J. (2020). Design thinking and virtual reality in the cruise industry. Master of Engineering [Online]. Avalaible at: https://www.theseus.fi/bitstream/handle/10024/337692/juha_hollanti.pdf?sequence=2.

Holyoak, K.J. (1985). The pragmatics of analogical transfer. *The Psychology of Learning and Motivation*, 19, 59–87.

Ibrahim, R. and Rahimian, F.P. (2010). Comparison of CAD and manual sketching tools for teaching architectural design. *Automation in Construction*, 19(8), 978–987.

ISO (2009). *DIS 9241-210: 2010. Ergonomics of Human System Interaction Part 210: Human-centred Design for Interactive Systems*. International Standardization Organization (ISO), Switzerland.

Jackson, B. and Keefe, D.F. (2016). Lift-off: Using reference imagery and freehand sketching to create 3D models in VR. *IEEE Transactions on Visualization and Computer Graphics*, 22(4), 1442–1451.

Jett, Q.R. and George, J.M. (2003). Work interrupted: A closer look at the role of interruptions in organizational life. *Academy of Management Review*, 28(3), 494–507.

Johnston, W.A., Hawley, K.J., Plewe, S.H., Elliott, J.M., DeWitt, M.J. (1990). Attention capture by novel stimuli. *Journal of Experimental Psychology: General*, 119(4), 397.

Kaplan, S. (1995). The restorative benefits of nature: Toward and integrative framework. *Journal of Environmental Psychology*, 15, 169–182.

Kaplan, R. and Kaplan, S. (1989). *The Experience of Nature: A Psychological Perspective*. Cambridge University Press, New York, USA.

Kasof, J. (1997). Creativity and breadth of attention. *Creativity Research Journal*, 10(4), 303–315.

Keum, D.D. and See, K.E. (2017). The influence of hierarchy on idea generation and selection in the innovation process. *Organization Science*, 28(4), 653–669.

Knight, A.P. and Baer, M. (2014). Get up, stand up: The effects of a non-sedentary workspace on information elaboration and group performance. *Social Psychological and Personality Science*, 5(8), 910–917.

Kohn, N.W. (2008). *An Examination of Fixation in Brainstorming*. Texas A&M University, College Station, TX, USA.

de Kort, Y.A., Meijnders, A.L., Sponselee, A.A., IJsselsteijn, W.A. (2006). What's wrong with virtual trees? Restoring from stress in a mediated environment. *Journal of Environmental Psychology*, 26(4), 309–320.

Kosmadoudi, Z., Lim, T., Ritchie, J., Louchart, S., Liu, Y., Sung, R. (2013). Engineering design using game-enhanced CAD: The potential to augment the user experience with game elements. *Computer-Aided Design*, 45(3), 777–795.

Kruger, J. and Dunning, D. (1999). Unskilled and unaware of it: How difficulties in recognizing one's own incompetence lead to inflated self-assessments. *Journal of Personality and Social Psychology*, 77, 1121–1134 [Online]. Available at: http://psycnet.apa.orgjournals/psp/77/6/1121.

Küper, M., Kaschani, P., Thürling, M., Stefanescu, M.R., Burciu, R.G., Göricke, S., Maderwald, S., Ladd, M.E., Hautzel, H., Timmann, D. (2016). Cerebellar fMRI activation increases with increasing working memory demands. *The Cerebellum*, 15(3), 322–335.

Kweon, B.S., Ulrich, R.S., Walker, V.D., Tassinary, L.G. (2008). Anger and stress: The role of landscape posters in an office setting. *Environment and Behavior*, 40(3), 355–381.

Lamm, H. and Trommsdorff, G. (1973). Group versus individual performance on tasks requiring ideational proficiency (brainstorming): A review. *European Journal of Social Psychology*, 3(4), 361–388.

Leather, P., Pyrgas, M., Beale, D., Lawrence, C. (1998). Windows in the workplace: Sunlight, view, and occupational stress. *Environment and Behavior*, 30(6), 739–762.

Lechtzin, N., Busse, A.M., Smith, M.T., Grossman, S., Nesbit, S., Diette, G.B. (2010). A randomized trial of nature scenery and sounds versus urban scenery and sounds to reduce pain in adults undergoing bone marrow aspirate and biopsy. *The Journal of Alternative and Complementary Medicine*, 16(9), 965–972.

Lecossier, A., Pallot, M., Crubleau, P., Richir, S. (2018). Towards radical innovations in a mature company: An empirical study on the UX-FFE model. *Artificial Intelligence for Engineering Design, Analysis and Manufacturing*, 33, 1–16.

Lecossier, A., Pallot, M., Crubleau, P., Richir, S. (2019). Construction of an instrument to evaluate the user eXperience of a group of co-creators in the upstream innovation process. *International Journal of Services Operations and Informatics*, 10(1), 17–42.

Lee, Y.S. (2016). Creative workplace characteristics and innovative start-up companies. *Facilities*, 34(7/8), 413–432.

Lee, K.E., Williams, K.J., Sargent, L.D., Williams, N.S., Johnson, K.A. (2015). 40-second green roof views sustain attention: The role of micro-breaks in attention restoration. *Journal of Environmental Psychology*, 42, 182–189.

Lee, J.H., Yang, E.K., Sun, Z.Y. (2019). Design cognitive actions stimulating creativity in the VR design environment. *Proceedings of the 2019 on Creativity and Cognition*, ACM, New York, USA, 604–611.

Lewandowsky, S. and Murdock Jr., B.B. (1989). Memory for serial order. *Psychological Review*, 96(1), 25.

Lin, J.J. and Parker, D.E. (2007). User experience modeling and enhancement for virtual environments that employ wide-field displays. *International Conference on Digital Human Modeling*. Springer, Heidelberg, 423–433.

MacDonald, R., Byrne, C., Carlton, L. (2006). Creativity and flow in musical composition: An empirical investigation. *Psychology of Music*, 34(3), 292–306.

Magadley, W. and Birdi, K. (2009). Innovation labs: An examination into the use of physical spaces to enhance organizational creativity. *Creativity and Innovation Management*, 18(4), 315–325.

Marchand, E., Dorta, T., Pierini, D. (2018). Influence of immersive contextual environments on collaborative ideation cognition – Through design conversations, gestures and sketches. *Proceedings of the 36th eCAADe Conference – Volume 2, Lodz University of Technology*, Łódź, Poland, 795–804, 19–21 September.

Marinussen, M. and de Rooij, A. (2019). Being yourself to be creative: How using self-similar avatars can support the generation of original ideas in virtual environments. *ACM Creativity and Cognition 2019*, Association for Computing Machinery, New York, USA.

Martens, Y. (2011). Creative workplace: Instrumental and symbolic support for creativity. *Facilities*, 29(1/2), 63–79.

Martin, R.C., Wogalter, M.S., Forlano, J.G. (1988). Reading comprehension in the presence of unattended speech and music. *Journal of Memory and Language*, 27(4), 382–398.

Mauborgne, R. and Kim, W.C. (2007). *Blue Ocean Strategy*. Gildan Media. Landover, MD, USA.

McCoy, J.M. and Evans, G.W. (2002). The potential role of the physical environment in fostering creativity. *Creativity Research Journal*, 14(3–4), 409–426.

McGlone, M.S. and Tofighbakhsh, J. (2000). Birds of a feather flock conjointly (?): Rhyme as reason in aphorisms. *Psychological Science*, 11(5), 424–428.

McKim, R. (ed.) (1980). Chapter 20. In *Experiences in Visual Thinking*. PWS, Boston, MA, USA.

Messinger, P.R., Ge, X., Stroulia, E., Lyons, K., Smirnov, K., Bone, M. (2008). On the relationship between my avatar and myself. *Journal for Virtual Worlds Research*, 1(2), 1–17.

Mille, C. (2020). Studies of cognitive factors linked to digital tools applied for the design upstream phases. Doctoral Dissertation.

Mille, C., Christmann, O., Fleury, S., Richir, S. (2020). Effects of digital tools feature on creativity and communicability of ideas for upstream phase of conception. *4th International Conference on Computer-Human Interaction Research and Applications*. INSTICC, SciTePress, Setúbal, Portugal.

Miller, G.A. (1956). The magical number seven, plus or minus two: Some limits on our capacity for processing information. *Psychological Review*, 63(2), 81.

Mochi, F. and Madjar, N. (2018). Chapter 5 – Interruptions and multitasking: Advantages and disadvantages for creativity at work. In *Individual Creativity in the Workplace, Explorations in Creativity Research*, Reiter-Palmon, R., Kennel, V.L., Kaufman, J.C. (eds). Academic Press, Cambridge, MA, USA.

Myers, I.B., McCaulley, M.H., Most, R. (1985). *Manual, a Guide to the Development and Use of the Myers-Briggs Type Indicator*. Consulting Psychologists Press. Palo Alto, CA, USA.

Nakagawa, M. (2005). On-line handwriting recognition for creativity human interfaces. *Proceedings of the International Workshop on Document Analysis (IWDA-05), Kolkata*, 31–52.

Nawrot, M. and Rizzo, M. (1995). Motion perception deficits from midline cerebellar lesions in human. *Vision Research*, 35(5), 723–731.

Norton, M.I., Mochon, D., Ariely, D. (2012). The IKEA effect: When labor leads to love. *Journal of Consumer Psychology*, 22(3), 453–460.

Oppezzo, M. and Schwartz, D.L. (2014). Give your ideas some legs: The positive effect of walking on creative thinking. *Journal of Experimental Psychology: Learning, Memory, and Cognition*, 40(4), 1142.

Oswald, M.E. and Grosjean, S. (2004). Confirmation bias. *Cognitive Illusions: A Handbook on Fallacies and Biases in Thinking, Judgement and Memory*. Psychology Press, Hove, United Kingdom.

Pelland, G., Ramirez, M.C., Grzybek, R.N. (2019). Application of virtual reality to the engineering design process. Report [Online]. Available at: https://digital.wpi.edu/pdfviewer/h702q9097.

Plambech, T. and Van Den Bosch, C.C.K. (2015). The impact of nature on creativity – A study among Danish creative professionals. *Urban Forestry & Urban Greening*, 14(2), 255–263.

Pronin, E. and Kugler, M.B. (2007). Valuing thoughts, ignoring behavior: The introspection illusion as a source of the bias blind spot. *Journal of Experimental Social Psychology*, 43(4), 565–578.

Raanaas, R.K., Evensen, K.H., Rich, D., Sjøstrøm, G., Patil, G. (2011). Benefits of indoor plants on attention capacity in an office setting. *Journal of Environmental Psychology*, 31(1), 99–105.

Ratan, R. and Hasler, B.S. (2014). Playing well with virtual classmates: Relating avatar design to group satisfaction. *Proceedings of the 17th ACM Conference on Computer Supported Cooperative Work and Social Computing*, ACM, New York, USA, 564–573.

Reitzig, M. and Sorenson, O. (2013). Biases in the selection stage of bottom-up strategy formulation. *Strategic Management Journal*, 34(7), 782–799.

Rieuf, V. (2013). Impact of the immersive experience on Kansei during the early industrial design. Doctoral dissertation, PhD thesis, ENSAM ParisTech, Paris.

Rieuf, V., Bouchard, C., Meyrueis, V., Omhover, J.F. (2017). Emotional activity in early immersive design: Sketches and moodboards in virtual reality. *Design Studies*, 48, 43–75.

Ritter, S.M. and Ferguson, S. (2017). Happy creativity: Listening to happy music facilitates divergent thinking. *PloS One*, 12(9), e0182210.

Robertson, B.F. and Radcliffe, D.F. (2009). Impact of CAD tools on creative problem solving in engineering design. *Computer-Aided Design*, 41(3), 136–146.

Rodgers, P.A., Green, G., Mcgown, A. (2000). Using concept sketches to track design progress. *Design Studies*, 21(5), 451–464.

de Rooij, A., Corr, P.J., Jones, S. (2015). Emotion and creativity: Hacking into cognitive appraisal processes to augment creative ideation. *Proceedings of the 2015 ACM SIGCHI Conference on Creativity and Cognition*, ACM, New York, USA, 265–274.

de Rooij, A., van der Land, S., van Erp, S. (2017). The creative Proteus effect: How self-similarity, embodiment, and priming of creative stereotypes with avatars influences creative ideation. *Proceedings of the 2017 ACM SIGCHI Conference on Creativity and Cognition*. ACM, 232–236.

Schön, D.A. (1983). *The Reflective Practitioner: How Professionals Think in Action*. Basic Books Inc, New York, USA.

Shah, J.J., Vargas-Hernandez, N.O.E., Summers, J.D., Kulkarni, S. (2001). Collaborative sketching (C-Sketch) – An idea generation technique for engineering design. *The Journal of Creative Behavior*, 35(3), 168–198.

Shibata, S. and Suzuki, N. (2004). Effects of an indoor plant on creative task performance and mood. *Scandinavian Journal of Psychology*, 45(5), 373–381.

Shina, D.H., Bioccab, F., Chooc, H. (2013). Exploring the user experience of three-dimensional virtual learning environments. *Behaviour & Information Technology*, 32, 203–214.

Steidle, A. and Werth, L. (2013). Freedom from constraints: Darkness and dim illumination promote creativity. *Journal of Environmental Psychology*, 35, 67–80.

Steiner, G. (2006). Innovative performance of organizations as a result of their physical environment. *XVIth World Congress on Sociology, "The Quality of Social Existence in a Globalistic World"*, July 23–29, Durban, South Africa.

Sternberg, R.J. (2006). The nature of creativity. *Creativity Research Journal*, 18(1), 87.

Stokols, D., Clitheroe, C., Zmuidzinas, M. (2002). Qualities of work environments that promote perceived support for creativity. *Creativity Research Journal*, 14(2), 137–147.

Stroebe, W., Nijstad, B.A., Rietzschel, E.F. (2010). Beyond productivity loss in brainstorming groups: The evolution of a question. In *Advances in Experimental Social Psychology*, Academic Press. Cambridge, MA, USA, 43, 157–203.

Sullivan, M. (2018). *Time Biases: A Theory of Rational Planning and Personal Persistence*. Oxford University Press. Oxford, United Kingdom.

Sung, S.Y. and Choi, J.N. (2009). Do Big Five personality factors affect individual creativity? The moderating role of extrinsic motivation. *Social Behavior and Personality: An International Journal*, 37(7), 941–956.

Tcha-Tokey, K., Christmann, O., Loup-Escande, E., Loup, G., and Richir, S. (2018). Towards a model of user experience in immersive virtual environments. *Advances in Human-Computer Interaction*, 7827286 [Online]. Available at: https://doi.org/10.1155/2018/7827286.

Toker, U. and Gray, D.O. (2008). Innovation spaces: Workspace planning and innovation in US university research centers. *Research Policy*, 37(2), 309–329.

Trompette, P., Chanal, V., Pelissier, C. (2008). Crowdsourcing as a way to access external knowledge for innovation: Control, incentive and coordination in hybrid forms of innovation. *24th EGOS Colloquium*, July, Amsterdam, The Netherlands.

Tseng, W.S. and Ball, L.J. (2011). How uncertainty helps sketch interpretation in a design task. In *Design Creativity 2010*, Taura, T., Nagai, Y. (eds). Springer, London, United Kingdom.

Tyrväinen, L., Ojala, A., Korpela, K., Lanki, T., Tsunetsugu, Y., Kagawa, T. (2014). The influence of urban green environments on stress relief measures: A field experiment. *Journal of Environmental Psychology*, 38, 1–9.

Ullman, D.G. (2003). *The Mechanical Design Process*, Volume 2. McGraw-Hill, New York, USA.

Ullman, D.G., Wood, S., Craig, D. (1990). The importance of drawing in the mechanical design process. *Computers & Graphics*, 14(2), 263–274.

Ulrich, R.S. (1981). Natural versus urban scenes: Some psychophysiological effects. *Environment and Behavior*, 13(5), 523–556.

Ulrich, R.S. (1984). View through a window may influence recovery. *Science*, 224(4647), 224–225.

Ulrich, R.S., Simons, R.F., Losito, B.D., Fiorito, E., Miles, M.A., Zelson, M. (1991). Stress recovery during exposure to natural and urban environments. *Journal of Environmental Psychology*, 11(3), 201–230.

Vaccaro, A.J. (1988). Personality clash. *Personnel Administrator*, 33, 88–92.

Valtchanov, D., Barton, K.R., Ellard, C. (2010). Restorative effects of virtual nature settings. *Cyberpsychology, Behavior, and Social Networking*, 13(5), 503–512.

Van den Berg, A.E., Koole, S.L., Van der Wulp, N.Y. (2003). Environmental preference and restoration: (How) are they related? *Journal of Environmental Psychology*, 23(2), 135–146.

Visser, W. (2006). *The Cognitive Artifacts of Designing*. Lawrence Erlbaum Associates, Inc. Mahwah, NJ, USA.

Wallas, G. (1926). *The Art of Thought*. Jonathan Cape, London, United Kingdom.

Wenzel, M. and Meinel, C. (2020). Prototyper: A virtual remote prototyping space. In *Design Thinking Research*, Meinel, C., Leifer, L. (eds). Springer, Cham.

Whitla, P. (2009). Crowdsourcing and its application in marketing activities. *Contemporary Management Research*, 5(1), 15–28.

Yang, E.K. and Lee, J.H. (2020). Cognitive impact of virtual reality sketching on designers' concept generation. *Digital Creativity*, 31(2), 1–16.

Yang, X., Lin, L., Cheng, P.Y., Yang, X., Ren, Y., Huang, Y.M. (2018). Examining creativity through a virtual reality support system. *Educational Technology Research and Development*, 66(5), 1231–1254.

Yee, N. and Bailenson, J. (2007). The Proteus effect: The effect of transformed self-representation on behavior. *Human Communication Research*, 33(3), 271–290.

Zhou, T. (2013). Understanding the effect of flow on user adoption of mobile games. *Personal and Ubiquitous Computing*, 17(4), 741–748.

Index

Other titles from

ISTE

in

Innovation, Entrepreneurship and Management

2021

ARCADE Jacques
Strategic Engineering (Innovation and Technology Set – Volume 11)

BÉRANGER Jérôme, RIZOULIÈRES Roland
The Digital Revolution in Health (Health and Innovation Set – Volume 2)

BOBILLIER CHAUMON Marc-Eric
Digital Transformations in the Challenge of Activity and Work: Understanding and Supporting Technological Changes (Technological Changes and Human Resources Set – Volume 3)

BUCLET Nicolas
Territorial Ecology and Socio-ecological Transition (Smart Innovation Set – Volume 34)

DIMOTIKALIS Yannis, KARAGRIGORIOU Alex, PARPOULA Christina, SKIADIS Christos H
Applied Modeling Techniques and Data Analysis 1: Computational Data Analysis Methods and Tools (Big Data, Artificial Intelligence and Data Analysis Set - Volume 7)
Applied Modeling Techniques and Data Analysis 2: Financial, Demographic, Stochastic and Statistical Models and Methods (Big Data, Artificial Intelligence and Data Analysis Set – Volume 8)

DISPAS Christophe, KAYANAKIS Georges, SERVEL Nicolas, STRIUKOVA Ludmila
Innovation and Financial Markets (Innovation between Risk and Reward Set – Volume 7)

ENJOLRAS Manon
Innovation and Export: The Joint Challenge of the Small Company (Smart Innovation Set – Volume 37)

GOGLIN Christian
Emotions and Values in Equity Crowdfunding Investment Choices 2: Modeling and Empirical Study

GRENIER Corinne, OIRY Ewan
Altering Frontiers: Organizational Innovations in Healthcare (Health and Innovation Set – Volume 1)

GUERRIER Claudine
Security and Its Challenges in the 21st Century (Innovation and Technology Set – Volume 12)

HELLER David
Performance of Valuation Methods in Financial Transactions (Modern Finance, Management Innovation and Economic Growth Set – Volume 4)

LEHMANN Paul-Jacques
Liberalism and Capitalism Today

SOULÉ Bastien, HALLÉ Julie, VIGNAL Bénédicte, BOUTROY Éric, NIER Olivier
Innovation Trajectories and Process Optimization (Smart Innovation Set – Volume 35)

UZUNIDIS Dimitri, KASMI Fedoua, ADATTO Laurent
Innovation Economics, Engineering and Management Handbook 1: Main Themes
Innovation Economics, Engineering and Management Handbook 2: Special Themes

VALLIER Estelle
Innovation in Clusters: Science–Industry Relationships in the Face of Forced Advancement (Smart Innovation Set – Volume 36)

2020

ACH Yves-Alain, RMADI-SAÏD Sandra
Financial Information and Brand Value: Reflections, Challenges and Limitations

ANDREOSSO-O'CALLAGHAN Bernadette, DZEVER Sam, JAUSSAUD Jacques, TAYLOR Robert
Sustainable Development and Energy Transition in Europe and Asia (Innovation and Technology Set – Volume 9)

BEN SLIMANE Sonia, M'HENNI Hatem
Entrepreneurship and Development: Realities and Future Prospects (Smart Innovation Set – Volume 30)

CHOUTEAU Marianne, FOREST Joëlle, NGUYEN Céline
Innovation for Society: The P.S.I. Approach (Smart Innovation Set – Volume 28)

CORON Clotilde
Quantifying Human Resources: Uses and Analysis (Technological Changes and Human Resources Set – Volume 2)

CORON Clotilde, GILBERT Patrick
Technological Change
(Technological Changes and Human Resources Set – Volume 1)

CERDIN Jean-Luc, PERETTI Jean-Marie
The Success of Apprenticeships: Views of Stakeholders on Training and Learning (Human Resources Management Set – Volume 3)

DELCHET-COCHET Karen
Circular Economy: From Waste Reduction to Value Creation
(Economic Growth Set – Volume 2)

DIDAY Edwin, GUAN Rong, SAPORTA Gilbert, WANG Huiwen
Advances in Data Science
(Big Data, Artificial Intelligence and Data Analysis Set – Volume 4)

DOS SANTOS PAULINO Victor
Innovation Trends in the Space Industry
(Smart Innovation Set – Volume 25)

GASMI Nacer
Corporate Innovation Strategies: Corporate Social Responsibility and Shared Value Creation
(Smart Innovation Set – Volume 33)

GOGLIN Christian
Emotions and Values in Equity Crowdfunding Investment Choices 1: Transdisciplinary Theoretical Approach

GUILHON Bernard
Venture Capital and the Financing of Innovation
(Innovation Between Risk and Reward Set – Volume 6)

LATOUCHE Pascal
Open Innovation: Human Set-up
(Innovation and Technology Set – Volume 10)

LIMA Marcos
Entrepreneurship and Innovation Education: Frameworks and Tools
(Smart Innovation Set – Volume 32)

MACHADO Carolina, DAVIM J. Paulo
Sustainable Management for Managers and Engineers

MAKRIDES Andreas, KARAGRIGORIOU Alex, SKIADAS Christos H.
Data Analysis and Applications 3: Computational, Classification, Financial, Statistical and Stochastic Methods
(Big Data, Artificial Intelligence and Data Analysis Set – Volume 5)
Data Analysis and Applications 4: Financial Data Analysis and Methods
(Big Data, Artificial Intelligence and Data Analysis Set – Volume 6)

MASSOTTE Pierre, CORSI Patrick
Complex Decision-Making in Economy and Finance

MEUNIER François-Xavier
Dual Innovation Systems: Concepts, Tools and Methods
(Smart Innovation Set – Volume 31)

MICHAUD Thomas
Science Fiction and Innovation Design (Innovation in Engineering and Technology Set – Volume 6)

MONINO Jean-Louis
Data Control: Major Challenge for the Digital Society
(Smart Innovation Set – Volume 29)

MORLAT Clément
Sustainable Productive System: Eco-development versus Sustainable Development (Smart Innovation Set – Volume 26)

SAULAIS Pierre, ERMINE Jean-Louis
Knowledge Management in Innovative Companies 2: Understanding and Deploying a KM Plan within a Learning Organization
(Smart Innovation Set – Volume 27)

2019

AMENDOLA Mario, GAFFARD Jean-Luc
Disorder and Public Concern Around Globalization

BARBAROUX Pierre
Disruptive Technology and Defence Innovation Ecosystems
(Innovation in Engineering and Technology Set – Volume 5)

DOU Henri, JUILLET Alain, CLERC Philippe
Strategic Intelligence for the Future 1: A New Strategic and Operational Approach
Strategic Intelligence for the Future 2: A New Information Function Approach

FRIKHA Azza
Measurement in Marketing: Operationalization of Latent Constructs

FRIMOUSSE Soufyane
Innovation and Agility in the Digital Age
(Human Resources Management Set – Volume 2)

GAY Claudine, SZOSTAK Bérangère L.
Innovation and Creativity in SMEs: Challenges, Evolutions and Prospects
(Smart Innovation Set – Volume 21)

GORIA Stéphane, HUMBERT Pierre, ROUSSEL Benoît
Information, Knowledge and Agile Creativity
(Smart Innovation Set – Volume 22)

HELLER David
Investment Decision-making Using Optional Models
(Economic Growth Set – Volume 2)

HELLER David, DE CHADIRAC Sylvain, HALAOUI Lana, JOUVET Camille
The Emergence of Start-ups
(Economic Growth Set – Volume 1)

HÉRAUD Jean-Alain, KERR Fiona, BURGER-HELMCHEN Thierry
Creative Management of Complex Systems
(Smart Innovation Set – Volume 19)

LATOUCHE Pascal
Open Innovation: Corporate Incubator
(Innovation and Technology Set – Volume 7)

LEHMANN Paul-Jacques
The Future of the Euro Currency

LEIGNEL Jean-Louis, MÉNAGER Emmanuel, YABLONSKY Serge
Sustainable Enterprise Performance: A Comprehensive Evaluation Method

LIÈVRE Pascal, AUBRY Monique, GAREL Gilles
Management of Extreme Situations: From Polar Expeditions to Exploration-Oriented Organizations

MILLOT Michel
Embarrassment of Product Choices 2: Towards a Society of Well-being

N'GOALA Gilles, PEZ-PÉRARD Virginie, PRIM-ALLAZ Isabelle
Augmented Customer Strategy: CRM in the Digital Age

NIKOLOVA Blagovesta
The RRI Challenge: Responsibilization in a State of Tension with Market Regulation
(Innovation and Responsibility Set – Volume 3)

PELLEGRIN-BOUCHER Estelle, ROY Pierre
Innovation in the Cultural and Creative Industries
(Innovation and Technology Set – Volume 8)

PRIOLON Joël
Financial Markets for Commodities

QUINIOU Matthieu
Blockchain: The Advent of Disintermediation

RAVIX Joël-Thomas, DESCHAMPS Marc
Innovation and Industrial Policies
(Innovation between Risk and Reward Set – Volume 5)

ROGER Alain, VINOT Didier
Skills Management: New Applications, New Questions
(Human Resources Management Set – Volume 1)

SAULAIS Pierre, ERMINE Jean-Louis
Knowledge Management in Innovative Companies 1: Understanding and Deploying a KM Plan within a Learning Organization
(Smart Innovation Set – Volume 23)

SERVAJEAN-HILST Romaric
Co-innovation Dynamics: The Management of Client-Supplier Interactions for Open Innovation
(Smart Innovation Set – Volume 20)

SKIADAS Christos H., BOZEMAN James R.
Data Analysis and Applications 1: Clustering and Regression, Modeling-estimating, Forecasting and Data Mining
(Big Data, Artificial Intelligence and Data Analysis Set – Volume 2)
Data Analysis and Applications 2: Utilization of Results in Europe and Other Topics
(Big Data, Artificial Intelligence and Data Analysis Set – Volume 3)

UZUNIDIS Dimitri
Systemic Innovation: Entrepreneurial Strategies and Market Dynamics

VIGEZZI Michel
World Industrialization: Shared Inventions, Competitive Innovations and Social Dynamics
(Smart Innovation Set – Volume 24)

2018

BURKHARDT Kirsten
Private Equity Firms: Their Role in the Formation of Strategic Alliances

CALLENS Stéphane
Creative Globalization
(Smart Innovation Set – Volume 16)

CASADELLA Vanessa
Innovation Systems in Emerging Economies: MINT – Mexico, Indonesia, Nigeria, Turkey
(Smart Innovation Set – Volume 18)

CHOUTEAU Marianne, FOREST Joëlle, NGUYEN Céline
Science, Technology and Innovation Culture
(Innovation in Engineering and Technology Set – Volume 3)

CORLOSQUET-HABART Marine, JANSSEN Jacques
Big Data for Insurance Companies
(Big Data, Artificial Intelligence and Data Analysis Set – Volume 1)

CROS Françoise
Innovation and Society
(Smart Innovation Set – Volume 15)

DEBREF Romain
Environmental Innovation and Ecodesign: Certainties and Controversies
(Smart Innovation Set – Volume 17)

DOMINGUEZ Noémie
SME Internationalization Strategies: Innovation to Conquer New Markets

ERMINE Jean-Louis
Knowledge Management: The Creative Loop
(Innovation and Technology Set – Volume 5)

GILBERT Patrick, BOBADILLA Natalia, GASTALDI Lise,
LE BOULAIRE Martine, LELEBINA Olga
Innovation, Research and Development Management

IBRAHIMI Mohammed
Mergers & Acquisitions: Theory, Strategy, Finance

LEMAÎTRE Denis
Training Engineers for Innovation

LÉVY Aldo, BEN BOUHENI Faten, AMMI Chantal
Financial Management: USGAAP and IFRS Standards
(Innovation and Technology Set – Volume 6)

MILLOT Michel
Embarrassment of Product Choices 1: How to Consume Differently

PANSERA Mario, OWEN Richard
Innovation and Development: The Politics at the Bottom of the Pyramid
(Innovation and Responsibility Set – Volume 2)

RICHEZ Yves
Corporate Talent Detection and Development

SACHETTI Philippe, ZUPPINGER Thibaud
New Technologies and Branding
(Innovation and Technology Set – Volume 4)

SAMIER Henri
Intuition, Creativity, Innovation

TEMPLE Ludovic, COMPAORÉ SAWADOGO Eveline M.F.W.
Innovation Processes in Agro-Ecological Transitions in Developing Countries
(Innovation in Engineering and Technology Set – Volume 2)

UZUNIDIS Dimitri
Collective Innovation Processes: Principles and Practices
(Innovation in Engineering and Technology Set – Volume 4)

VAN HOOREBEKE Delphine
The Management of Living Beings or Emo-management

2017

AÏT-EL-HADJ Smaïl
The Ongoing Technological System
(Smart Innovation Set – Volume 11)

BAUDRY Marc, DUMONT Béatrice
Patents: Prompting or Restricting Innovation?
(Smart Innovation Set – Volume 12)

BÉRARD Céline, TEYSSIER Christine
Risk Management: Lever for SME Development and Stakeholder Value Creation

CHALENÇON Ludivine
Location Strategies and Value Creation of International Mergers and Acquisitions

CHAUVEL Danièle, BORZILLO Stefano
The Innovative Company: An Ill-defined Object
(Innovation between Risk and Reward Set – Volume 1)

CORSI Patrick
Going Past Limits To Growth

D'ANDRIA Aude, GABARRET Inés
Building 21st Century Entrepreneurship
(Innovation and Technology Set – Volume 2)

DAIDJ Nabyla
Cooperation, Coopetition and Innovation
(Innovation and Technology Set – Volume 3)

FERNEZ-WALCH Sandrine
The Multiple Facets of Innovation Project Management
(Innovation between Risk and Reward Set – Volume 4)

FOREST Joëlle
Creative Rationality and Innovation
(Smart Innovation Set – Volume 14)

GUILHON Bernard
Innovation and Production Ecosystems
(Innovation between Risk and Reward Set – Volume 2)

HAMMOUDI Abdelhakim, DAIDJ Nabyla
Game Theory Approach to Managerial Strategies and Value Creation
(Diverse and Global Perspectives on Value Creation Set – Volume 3)

LALLEMENT Rémi
Intellectual Property and Innovation Protection: New Practices and New Policy Issues
(Innovation between Risk and Reward Set – Volume 3)

LAPERCHE Blandine
Enterprise Knowledge Capital
(Smart Innovation Set – Volume 13)

LEBERT Didier, EL YOUNSI Hafida
International Specialization Dynamics
(Smart Innovation Set – Volume 9)

MAESSCHALCK Marc
Reflexive Governance for Research and Innovative Knowledge
(Responsible Research and Innovation Set – Volume 6)

MASSOTTE Pierre
Ethics in Social Networking and Business 1: Theory, Practice and Current Recommendations
Ethics in Social Networking and Business 2: The Future and Changing Paradigms

MASSOTTE Pierre, CORSI Patrick
Smart Decisions in Complex Systems

MEDINA Mercedes, HERRERO Mónica, URGELLÉS Alicia
Current and Emerging Issues in the Audiovisual Industry
(Diverse and Global Perspectives on Value Creation Set – Volume 1)

MICHAUD Thomas
Innovation, Between Science and Science Fiction
(Smart Innovation Set – Volume 10)

PELLÉ Sophie
Business, Innovation and Responsibility
(Responsible Research and Innovation Set – Volume 7)

SAVIGNAC Emmanuelle
The Gamification of Work: The Use of Games in the Workplace

SUGAHARA Satoshi, DAIDJ Nabyla, USHIO Sumitaka
Value Creation in Management Accounting and Strategic Management: An Integrated Approach
(Diverse and Global Perspectives on Value Creation Set –Volume 2)

UZUNIDIS Dimitri, SAULAIS Pierre
Innovation Engines: Entrepreneurs and Enterprises in a Turbulent World (Innovation in Engineering and Technology Set – Volume 1)

2016

BARBAROUX Pierre, ATTOUR Amel, SCHENK Eric
Knowledge Management and Innovation (Smart Innovation Set – Volume 6)

BEN BOUHENI Faten, AMMI Chantal, LEVY Aldo
Banking Governance, Performance And Risk-Taking: Conventional Banks Vs Islamic Banks

BOUTILLIER Sophie, CARRÉ Denis, LEVRATTO Nadine
Entrepreneurial Ecosystems (Smart Innovation Set – Volume 2)

BOUTILLIER Sophie, UZUNIDIS Dimitri
The Entrepreneur (Smart Innovation Set – Volume 8)

BOUVARD Patricia, SUZANNE Hervé
Collective Intelligence Development in Business

GALLAUD Delphine, LAPERCHE Blandine
Circular Economy, Industrial Ecology and Short Supply Chains (Smart Innovation Set – Volume 4)

GUERRIER Claudine
Security and Privacy in the Digital Era (Innovation and Technology Set – Volume 1)

MEGHOUAR Hicham
Corporate Takeover Targets

MONINO Jean-Louis, SEDKAOUI Soraya
Big Data, Open Data and Data Development (Smart Innovation Set – Volume 3)

MOREL Laure, LE ROUX Serge
Fab Labs: Innovative User (Smart Innovation Set – Volume 5)

PICARD Fabienne, TANGUY Corinne
Innovations and Techno-ecological Transition
(Smart Innovation Set – Volume 7)

2015

CASADELLA Vanessa, LIU Zeting, DIMITRI Uzunidis
Innovation Capabilities and Economic Development in Open Economies
(Smart Innovation Set – Volume 1)

CORSI Patrick, MORIN Dominique
Sequencing Apple's DNA

CORSI Patrick, NEAU Erwan
Innovation Capability Maturity Model

FAIVRE-TAVIGNOT Bénédicte
Social Business and Base of the Pyramid

GODÉ Cécile
Team Coordination in Extreme Environments

MAILLARD Pierre
Competitive Quality and Innovation

MASSOTTE Pierre, CORSI Patrick
Operationalizing Sustainability

MASSOTTE Pierre, CORSI Patrick
Sustainability Calling

2014

DUBÉ Jean, LEGROS Diègo
Spatial Econometrics Using Microdata

LESCA Humbert, LESCA Nicolas
Strategic Decisions and Weak Signals

2013

HABART-CORLOSQUET Marine, JANSSEN Jacques, MANCA Raimondo
VaR Methodology for Non-Gaussian Finance

2012

DAL PONT Jean-Pierre
Process Engineering and Industrial Management

MAILLARD Pierre
Competitive Quality Strategies

POMEROL Jean-Charles
Decision-Making and Action

SZYLAR Christian
UCITS Handbook

2011

LESCA Nicolas
Environmental Scanning and Sustainable Development

LESCA Nicolas, LESCA Humbert
Weak Signals for Strategic Intelligence: Anticipation Tool for Managers

MERCIER-LAURENT Eunika
Innovation Ecosystems

2010

SZYLAR Christian
Risk Management under UCITS III/IV

2009

COHEN Corine
Business Intelligence

ZANINETTI Jean-Marc
Sustainable Development in the USA

2008

CORSI Patrick, DULIEU Mike
The Marketing of Technology Intensive Products and Services

DZEVER Sam, JAUSSAUD Jacques, ANDREOSSO Bernadette
Evolving Corporate Structures and Cultures in Asia: Impact of Globalization

2007

AMMI Chantal
Global Consumer Behavior

2006

BOUGHZALA Imed, ERMINE Jean-Louis
Trends in Enterprise Knowledge Management

CORSI Patrick *et al.*
Innovation Engineering: the Power of Intangible Networks

Printed and bound by CPI Group (UK) Ltd, Croydon, CR0 4YY
15/09/2026
14962408-0001